PASSED THROUGH FIRE

ONE WOMAN'S ESCAPE OUT OF A "CHRISTIAN" CULT

JAMIE SAGERSER

Edited by

CAROLYN RICE

I dedicate this book first and foremost to my beautiful children, grandchildren, and future generations. I also dedicate this book to all women and children who have suffered abuse. My prayer is that you will find hope within these pages.

May the Lord Jesus Bless you and keep you!

CONTENTS

PASSED THROUGH FIRE

FOREWORD

"Drawn from the water." Moses' name bore his testimony of a childhood deliverance from peril and death. I've wondered if Moses pondered much the fact that he was one of the few survivors of his generation, a generation that was killed due to the wrath of a wicked king.

To be spared from a generational decree "Every son that is born to the Hebrews you shall cast into the Nile..." (Exodus 1:22 NIV) because of the courage and faith of his mother; to be put into the same waters that drowned countless other children, held above and preserved from death, afloat, only because of the covering of God's gracious basket. This was Moses' beginning. This was also my beginning.

The testimony shared in this book is one of difficulty, a journey out of deep deception. It is about a woman who heard the whisper of God's inviting voice in the midst of hurricanes and floods. A woman who showed by her actions the meaning of faith, being sure of what she hoped for and evidencing the unseen. This woman was weak, timid, easily pushed around by ungodly men; and yet God used the weak of this world to shame the strong. He called out a broken woman and established her to show the unfailing nature of

His promises towards those He loves. I hope as you read this book and turn these pages you will see the God of infinite mercy, the One who has promised "I will never leave you nor forsake you," (Hebrews 13:5 NIV) I hope you will be challenged to start saying "yes" to Him.

A difficulty I have faced in my life is the humbling question of "Why me?" I was only a child, not innocent by any means, and yet carried out of bondage; somehow counted among God's refugees fleeing in the wilderness. Many people confused and angry at unanswered questions, refuse to surrender to the Lord because they can't understand the "why's" of life.

Why did this one die while the other lived, why were these given opportunities when the others had none, why would God allow this or not stop that?

These questions are not new. The men of Jesus day even asked Him such questions recorded in Luke 13. The answer God gives us is this: repent. I cannot give the reasons why I was spared as a child, why I was sheltered and protected by the Lord, but there is one thing I am confident of, the very same call to repentance that fell upon my mother (that falls upon all people in all places) has fallen upon me. My mother chose to give up her life for Christ, to take up her cross and follow Him; I too must make those hard choices. Although I have been offered freedom, I must *choose* to walk in it. It is not enough that I simply enjoy the freedoms that others have fought for.

We all walk in the footsteps of giants of the faith, men and woman who have walked out such pain and difficulty, to declare and pass down the Gospel of hope and life, a Gospel that invades and transcends this world, yet the promise is always stated in the present, "Today if you hear his voice do not harden your hearts..." (Hebrews 3:15 NIV) I pray that this testimony will encourage your testimony, and your testimony will encourage the next generation, until all hear of the glories of Christ and His bride is prepared for His return.

Joshua Sawyer
Tamara's youngest son

INTRODUCTION

You know that place between sleep and awake?

From here I look out, past my warm comforter, onto the icy waters surrounding me. I turn on the flashlight in my hand, scanning the surface, searching for bodies. I'm in a lifeboat, a crew mate from the Titanic. The wreckage from the shipwreck is sprawled before me. Breathing in shards of icy air becomes more painful as I take in the scene.

So much death.

In desperation I call out to any survivors! As passengers float past me, I grab them, leaning precariously out of the boat, caring not about the risk. I know I am to extend my hand, but at the same time aware that God alone can revive them.

How do I know? Because I too survived a mighty shipwreck; losing everything, including the only life I had ever known.

This book is an invitation for you to come with me, as I share my story of not only surviving, but overcoming a "Christian" cult, incest, witchcraft, alcoholism, drugs, physical and spiritual abuse.

"And they burned their sons and their daughters as offerings and used divination and omens and sold themselves to do evil in the sight of the LORD, provoking him to anger." *~2 Kings 17:17 NIV*

May this book bring Glory to the one and only Savior, Jesus Christ, our Lord.

CHAPTER 1

The cords of death entangled me; the torrents of destruction
overwhelmed me. The cords of the grave coiled around me; the
snares of death confronted me. In my distress I called to the LORD;
I cried to my God for help. From his temple he heard my voice; my
cry came before him, into his ears. ~Psalm 18:4-6 NIV

PRESENT 1989

"WHAT ARE YOU UP TO?" BRENT'S DARK VOICE JOLTED TAMARA
from her reading.

Shifting in his chair at the dining room table, his stainless-steel
knife tapped the plate piled high with the food she had meticulously
prepared. Turning his head sharply, neck muscles taut, he leaned
into the living room where she sat.

"Nothing," she swallowed hard, *how could he possibly know?* "Why
would you ask that?" Trembling, her fingers pressed white upon her
black leather Bible.

Brent's crystal blue eyes pierced her, eyes no longer his own. A dark being seemed to have pushed its way to the forefront of her husband's soul. The eyes were searching, trying to detect what was truly going on.

Unnerved, all Tamara could do was silently pray. The evil spirit tried to see through her but could not move past the Holy Spirit within. It felt much like the alien movies she'd seen, the aliens sent out probes as it were, to detect human life. To not only detect it, but destroy it.

His penetrating gaze finally broke, and he returned to slathering butter on his roll.

Tamara hastened to the kitchen, refilling his glass of milk, attempting to meet unspoken needs, preventing any flares of rage.

Her attention turned to scrubbing the pots and pans soaking in the sink. As she wiped a soapy spray of water off the kitchen window, she caught her reflection.

Jade green eyes reflected back in fear, she mustn't give way to it!

By all appearances it was another normal evening for their family, with Brent working the graveyard shift. Their boys had already been routinely fed and tucked into bed, long before Brent emerged from his room, much like a disgruntled bear roused prematurely from hibernation.

Whew! She knew she had dodged a bullet. She was already paranoid that her husband of eleven years would find the closet in her son's room stacked high with their suitcases.

Understanding that Brent was capable of murder if he suspected that she was leaving him for good kept her senses on high alert. He had even described what he would do to his family when she had threatened divorce. He painted a picture with his words in horrifying detail; Tamara and her son's lying in pools of blood, dead.

She drew in a deep breath as she added more soap to the dishwater tackling another greasy pan. No *matter how much I scrub, it seems there is a deeper layer to get to, more dirt...* her thoughts trailed off.

The adorable white ducks marching around the periwinkle blue border of her country kitchen seemed to mock her. No matter how she prayed for her proverbial ducks to be in a row, her world remained in chaos.

She had no idea of what lay ahead. She only knew that she had to get off the family mountain.

Tonight, had to be the night. When Brent left for work as usual, they would make a run for it; a run for freedom, a run for their very lives!

CHAPTER 2

Before them fire devours, behind them a flame blazes
Before them the land is like the garden of Eden, behind them, a
desert waste—
nothing escapes them. ~Joel 2:3 NIV

Brent wasn't gone more than fifteen minutes when Tamara heard her sister Terri's Silver Forerunner roar into the driveway.

Her brother Anthony hopped out and ran up to the front door, "Come quickly, Tamara, what if he comes back!"

They were all terrified of Brent, an ex-Army man who had sworn Tamara would be dead before she'd be free of him. He made it very clear that he owned Tamara. He'd nearly killed a man years before for flirting with her.

Tamara knew that her sister feared for her own life as well, as her husband Ray's rage equaled that of Brent's. Once he realized that she'd taken both of their girls, he too, would be hot on their trail.

They gathered up Tamara's three sleeping sons, Brandon,

Aaron and Joshua.

"Where are we going Mommy?" asked one of her boys, now rousing from his sleep.

"We're going to Disneyland! Won't that be fun?" she replied.

Her heart ached, as she knew that she was uprooting her children from their school and home, but knew deep down they would die if they stayed.

Now, bright eyed with excitement, the boys and their cousins Annie and Alicia chattered excitedly in the backseat.

It was true at that moment, Tamara fully intended on taking them to Disneyland. Her brother Anthony had come into town from California and was going to bring Tamara, Terri and their children back with him to live and begin a new life.

A fresh start away from that dark mountain was exactly what they needed. Walton's mountain, wasn't that what outsiders had laughingly dubbed it? Forty acres of beautifully forested land had been divided up so that Tamara and her siblings would each have a place to build homes, raise their children, and someday survive the end of the world, or in the terminology of their church, the "End Times."

People envied them.

If only they knew.

Tamara was crushed that their oldest sister Becky stayed in denial of the cult they were in. No matter how much she pleaded with her to look at the truth, Becky admonished her, and stood loyally by their parents. Tamara could not even say goodbye, as she knew that her sister would sound the alarm.

"The door won't shut!" Terri yelled. It was a brand-new vehicle and there was nothing in the way, yet it was as if an invisible force stopped it from closing.

There they were, tearing out of the driveway with the driver's door wide open.

"Lord Jesus!" they cried in unison, "Help us!"

Suddenly the door slammed shut.

Shaken, they headed down the mountain praying fervently for God's protection.

CHAPTER 3

What agreement is there between the temple of God and idols? For
we are the temple of the living God. As God has said: "I will live
with them and walk among them, and I will be their God, and they
will be my people. "Therefore, "Come out from them and be
separate, says the Lord. Touch no unclean thing, and I will receive
you. ~2 Corinthians 6:16-17 NIV

HOW HAD IT COME TO THIS? WHAT CRAZINESS, WHAT INSANITY HAD
engulfed their homes? They had seemingly run out of options with
nowhere to turn. It had been a few years since all hell had broken
loose. Tamara all too vividly recalled the prayer times led by her
mother Victoria.

PAST *1986*

FOR ENDLESS HOURS THEY MET TOGETHER, SHE AND HER SIBLINGS,

trying to make sense of a shattered world. It had all begun the day Victoria stepped over the threshold of a non-denominational Spirit-filled church. Tamara could see that her mother was at the end of her rope and desperate for answers. Victoria shared her feelings of hopelessness with Tamara.

"I have cried out to God for all of these years but your father doesn't change Tamara. He may have the respect of that Baptist church, but they don't know the home devil!"

"I'm so sorry Mom, I don't know what to say, the only thing I do know is that we need to keep praying for him." Tamara replied empathetically.

"I found a little church over on Fourth Plain Blvd, it says it is a Spirit filled assembly. I don't know much about them, I just can't do church as we have known it anymore. I am tired of feeling powerless. If God doesn't meet me there, I am filing for a divorce!"

Word of mouth spread quickly among the family about the new church. Victoria looked happy for the first time in years. God was indeed alive and listening, Oh, how they rejoiced!

Well, everyone, but Sam.

Tamara watched her father squirm as the Pastor seemed to be reading the family's mail.

Caught in the crossfire of Scripture laden arguments over breakfast after church, Tamara became convinced that her dad cooperated with attendance only to keep her mother from leaving him.

Sam vehemently disagreed with Victoria about how the supernatural gifts were being displayed and taught to the congregation, and had an arsenal of Bible verses to back up his view.

The staunch religious view that Victoria was fleeing.

What fun it was, despite the fierce opposition, to explore this new supernatural world, seeing and experiencing things Tamara and her family had never known before.

What started out so good soon took a dark turn. It was as if they boarded the Peter Pan ride at Disneyland and got off in the Haunted Mansion.

CHAPTER 4

Present 1989

Still visibly shaken, Terri maneuvered the SUV down the winding mountain roads. Darkness clung to the windows, a desperate attempt to obscure her view.

"What if *we're* the ones that are crazy?" Anthony's voice cracked, breaking the icy silence.

Tamara's retort came quickly, "We are *not* crazy, we know Mom went nuts seeking more power, Dad is evil incarnate and Terri and I married men just like him!"

Terri broke in without missing a beat, "And what about Pastor Garvin from your church, Tamara? Reaching out to him was a joke! Boy was he deluded, blithely telling us to forgive and move on!"

Anthony piped in, "Yeah, and even when you shared the

physical evidence about Terri's abuse with Mom's Pastor, he passed it off as Terri trying to pin her sexual sin on a good man!"

"Shush!" Tamara strained her neck to look around at the kids, now fast asleep, "We have to be careful of what the kids might overhear."

She leaned her aching head into a pillow shared by her precious son's sleeping head, *All I ever wanted was to serve Jesus and have peace,* she thought.

The more Tamara cried out for truth, the more her world blew apart. She quietly mouthed a line from her favorite worship song about God removing *all* that stood in the way of His love. One that had sung from her heart for years, not realizing that God was answering it, as if a prayer.

~

PAST (1971)

THE FIRST BIG CHANGES IN THEIR FAMILY BEGAN WHEN THEY STARTED attending church. Sam, a chronic alcoholic, checked into a rehabilitation center, and was supposedly on his way to becoming clean and sober. On the heels of finishing the program, he found a conservative Baptist church. A Bible believing body of believer's that held to a form of godliness, but denied the power of the Holy Spirit.

Gone were the days of the drunken orgies in their home out in the demonic woods and Tamara was beyond thrilled! She came with the hope of a child and believed church life would bring her one step closer to being accepted and loved by her father. As it turned out, the cloak of a Pharisee hid his flask of whiskey well. The wolf was fully received into the new flock, and he became a beloved Bible study teacher.

A traveling evangelist visited their sleepy little Baptist church, bringing with him an invitation to Heaven. Although she was eleven years old, it wasn't anything she had ever known before. Even in her church. The call from the Throne of God was beyond description. She felt unconditionally loved, accepted, and knew she had done nothing to deserve it.

What she thought she deserved was the beating for being so sinful!

~

THE BLOODY LASHING SHE'D SUFFERED IN MIDDLE SCHOOL WAS FOR passing a dirty picture to another student. She was called into the Principal's office, along with her parents.

The 20 mile drive out of town to their mountain home was dizzying with fear. Turning off the pavement onto the long and winding driveway made the back hairs of Tamara's neck stand up. She knew it drew her nearer to torture, her screams muffled by thick forest. She would pay dearly for exposing some of the darkness of their home.

Entering the house, her father headed for the leather hunting belt that hung ominously in the foyer closet. Her choice in clothing that morning turned out to be a terrible mistake.

Lapsing in and out of consciousness, she writhed on the floor, attempts to pull her skirt down thwarted by blows wrapping around her hands.

She feared she might die, yet wished she would.

Through the fog, Tamara heard her mother pleading, "Stop, you'll kill her!"

Tamara could not tell how much time elapsed before it actually stopped, or how long she lay on that floor after her parents left the room.

For weeks afterward each time she used the bathroom, she was reminded by the gashes so far up her leg that using the bathroom was excruciating.

She bore the marks on her body for some time, but the marks on her soul never went away. The beatings never removed sin from her. She felt that she *was* sin.

One of the deepest scars was that her mother, although pleading at one point, did nothing to help her!

Yes, she cried, *but she never made it stop.*

～

JESUS SOUGHT HER, AND FOUND HER IN THAT CHURCH MEETING. THE beatings that Jesus took on the cross, his lashings, were the only thing that could remove sin from Tamara. By His stripes, she could be healed.

Tamara felt like an orphan sitting in a pew, until her Heavenly Father adopted her. It would be many years before she could walk out of that dark and twisted world, but the King of Kings had left His tender mark on her that day, *This one's mine.*

CHAPTER 5

The Spirit clearly says that in later times some will abandon the
faith and follow deceiving spirits and things taught by demons.
~ 1 Timothy 4:1 NIV

PRESENT 1989

RACING DOWN THE HIGHWAY, THE SHOCKING REALITY OF LEAVING
the only life they had ever known was staggering, but they knew they
couldn't turn back.

As they talked of starting their new life in Los Angeles, out of
nowhere, what could only be described as a large black ball with a
serpentine tail came hurtling out of the cobalt sky toward their
vehicle.

"It's going to hit us!!" Tamara screamed.

Once again, her cry for Jesus' help rose from her innermost
being. The black sphere bounced off, inches from the driver's side
windshield, as if hitting an invisible barrier.

Shaken to the core, she prayed, begging for a reprieve from the agonizing terror that pursued them.

Long into the night, all quieted down except an occasional passing car on the long stretch of highway.

Tamara started to nod off when Terri's voice startled her awake.

The back hairs of her neck rose as she listened to her sister prophesy doom. "I just had a vision of Brent and Ray breaking into Anthony's apartment and murdering all of us!"

"What? Oh, Lord Jesus, where can we go?" Tamara prayed.

Fear thickened the air, choking them. Tamara rolled down the window as if to relieve it, when a huge black vulture appeared, the headlights catching it just for a moment.

"Look at that!" she cried.

"Oh my gosh!" gasped her sister Terri.

Anthony confirmed it was not the girl's imaginations, he had seen it too!

It was as if death taunted them, vultures at the ready to encircle their unmarked graves. They were truly in no man's land where no one knew them, and they barely knew themselves. Everything and everyone they had ever known was steeped in lies. Once again, they feverishly petitioned Heaven for help.

A spiritual horde of evil followed them, breathing down their necks, threatening to overtake them. But, was God's love as strong as death like the Bible proclaimed?

CHAPTER 6

For you know that it was not with perishable things such as silver or
gold that you were redeemed from the empty way of life handed
down to you from your ancestors.
~1 Peter 1:18 NIV

PAST (TAMARA'S CHILDHOOD MEMORY, 12 YEARS OLD 1972)

A SPIRIT OF DEATH HOVERED OVER TAMARA AND HER FAMILY AS FAR
back as she could remember. Victoria befriended a woman named
Doris, who was married with two daughters. They were all very
strange and mysterious. There was an eerie excitement whenever
they came over for dinner.

Whenever the couples got together, the children played in other
rooms unsupervised for hours. Doris' girls, Lucy and Carmen,
always insisted that the lights be turned out to tell scary stories by
candlelight.

The stories progressed to practicing levitation. The children were instructed by the oldest, Lucy, to surround one volunteer laid out on the floor, and hold out two fingers each, underneath the body. Before they knew it, they could lift them! They were amazed!

Eventually, they brought over an Ouija board and asked questions for the spirit world to answer. Tamara was titillated, but fearful.

Victoria came home one day and announced to the family that they would not be seeing Doris or her family ever again.

"Why Mom?" Tamara asked.

"Today I found out that Doris is a witch, she stays up all night with candles surrounding her living room and communicates with the dead." Victoria drew in a deep breath and continued. "Her husband is in the hospital. Doris told me the Ouija board foretold that something terrible was going to happen to him. The next day a steel door fell on him at work and broke both his legs!"

Tamara shuddered at the thought of what they had been doing. There was more to this seemingly innocent and spooky fun.

She was glad her mother shut the door to that world.

Or had she?

One evening she awakened, like many nights, startled.

Her eyes tried to focus in the moonlight, and spinning black discs swooshed round her, dark beings sat atop them but soon melted into shadows moving across the walls.

She called out to her sister, "Becky!"

Sharing a room with her older sibling brought little comfort. Nonetheless, she needed another human being awake to somehow fight off the other worldly predators.

"What now?" came her sister's groggy response.

"Some demons are in the room again!" cried Tamara.

Becky popped up as Tamara pointed. The manifestations were gone, but the tangible fear was not.

Tamara looked to her sister, begging for some reassurance of surviving the night, but all Becky offered was more evidence as to why they were not safe. "Remember a couple weeks ago when that black knight rode a horse into our room and pierced that wall with his sword?"

"Yeah." Tamara recalled it vividly.

The nightmare was so real that when they got up the next morning, the wall revealed a hole in the exact location her sister described. The hole was not there the day before.

The girls talked until morning light, too frightened to make their way to the light switch by the door. The thought of Tamara waking her parents never entered her mind. Disrupting their sleep was not an option. She knew she would be met with anger, scolded for being ridiculous, and ordered back to bed.

CHAPTER 7

Thinking he was in their company, they traveled on for a day. Then
they began looking for him among their relatives and friends.
~Luke 2:44 NIV

PRESENT 1989

NO MATTER WHAT EACH NEW DAY HELD, TAMARA'S MIND
continually tried to comprehend all she had experienced, to make
sense of madness. In her pursuit of Christ, she had by faith,
believed He was in their company. But when she looked for His
likeness among her relatives and friends, she could not find Him.

The truth was, He pursued them, wanting them to repent and
come to the truth. But they would not. They refused to lose their
way of life to find the true Christ.

The scariest thought plagued her *"To think Christ was in your
company your entire life, only to stand before the throne of God one day and hear*

Jesus say; 'I never knew you. Away from me, you evildoers!' Matthew 7:23 (NIV)

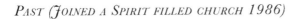

PAST (JOINED A SPIRIT FILLED CHURCH 1986)

TAMARA OBSERVED HER MOTHER ADVANCING IN LEAPS AND BOUNDS IN the spiritual new world of wonders. Having come out of a church where women were long suppressed by men, Victoria rejoiced in her new found freedom.

The Pastor's wife Jo practically danced up the aisle to greet Tamara. The joy in Jo's eyes fascinated her. A Christian who was happy*?*

Tamara wanted this joy!

After a few visits, Tamara made an appointment with Jo.

They met for lunch at Jo's house. Tamara sipped her tea, listening intently to her new friend tell of the wonders of God. She had heard many stories of the Bible over her lifetime, but none like this. The stories were alive. *Jo* was alive.

"I want to know Jesus like you!" Tamara said giddily.

"Well then, are you ready to receive the Holy Spirit?" asked Jo.

"Yes!" Tamara exclaimed.

The prayer for the Baptism of the Spirit was the easy part. When Jo asked Tamara to praise God with her in her new heavenly language, fear gripped her. She had been told that tongues were of the devil. Jo led her in a prayer to combat the fear.

With tears escaping her eyes, Tamara prayed a promise from Matthew, chapter 7, "If I ask for bread, you will not give me a stone, if I ask for a fish, you will not give me a serpent."

She did not speak in another language that day, but her breakthrough came the following weekend.

AFTER A HORRIBLE FIGHT WITH HER HUSBAND, TAMARA SAT ON THE edge of the bathtub, doubled over in gut wrenching pain. She groaned, like a woman in labor, and her spiritual language was birthed. It brought the relief she longed for, but opened her eyes to what she had been born into, a wicked lineage of darkness.

It would only be a matter of time before Victoria would rise up, proclaiming herself a "Prophetess."

Many nights Tamara and her sister were called by their mother to join prayer meetings at their mountain home. Victoria's prayer language became more and more loud and aggressive, scaring Tamara witless.

"Mother, why does your language sound so evil?" Tamara asked.

"I am engaged in spiritual warfare Tamara; I am fighting demons!" she retorted.

Still uncomfortable, Tamara continued in her own prayer language, pleading the blood of Jesus over herself, to keep from bolting away from the room at full speed. There was so much she needed to learn about this new realm, the Kingdom of God.

Victoria was more than happy to teach her.

At times they spent the night at their mother's home, as the prayer meetings went until 3 or 4 in the morning. They often awakened to strange happenings.

One time a large black bird strutted around their family room, with no open door or windows to have let it in, at least physically.

Another morning after an all-night prayer vigil, their sister Becky found human feces on top of the dryer in the laundry room.

Victoria always had an explanation, "This is retaliation of the kingdom of darkness! We are breaking strongholds and gaining ground for God, so of course the evil spirits are stirred up and angry!"

Going to sleep became something they had to spiritually prepare for. Pandora's box had been opened. The shadows they saw as children now took on forms.

∼

ONE EVENING IN TAMARA'S HOME, SHE SAT READING HER BIBLE, crying out deeply to God, to surrender all, to know Him more. As she drifted off to sleep next to her husband Brent, she was startled half-awake by a hand thrown down on the end of their waterbed, the wave rolling underneath her body.

She groggily sat up, and saw that an adorable, blonde haired child was slowly approaching her. In confusion as to who this could be in the middle of the night in her room, she held out her hand to him. The child opened his mouth and let out a demonic growl that snapped her fully awake and shook her to the core!

The wicked manifestation disappeared, and along with it, Tamara's desire to go deeper with spiritual pursuits. She put away her Bible and went out with friends, having a few drinks and dancing. Attending church on Sunday only was enough for most people. If she stayed ignorant of the supernatural world, like the majority, she hoped she wouldn't be attacked any further. Maybe the enemy would back off. She wanted to be with Christian people who were *normal*.

Only, the enemy did not back off.

Tamara didn't belong to this world, but she was also afraid of the spiritual realm. Satan had her blocked coming and going. Fear was a stronghold over her life. She could see no way to move forward.

CHAPTER 8

They are the kind who worm their way into homes and gain control over gullible women, who are loaded down with sins and are swayed by all kinds of evil desires, always learning but never able to come to a knowledge of the truth. ~2 Timothy 3:6-7 NIV

Past (Brent and Tamara, High School 1976)

TAMARA HAD BEEN QUITE TAKEN WITH BRENT SINCE HIGH SCHOOL, he was handsome and popular. He was an exceptional athlete and she'd fantasized about him while watching him play football, but felt that he was far beyond her reach. He had his pick of any of the girls in school.

When she turned 16, she ran away from home to go to a beach party an hour away and was the lucky girl who got to ride with Brent and his friend. He had broken up with his girlfriend and Tamara was the perfect rebound. She was hungry for attention and gave herself over to him without reservation. She surrendered every part of herself that night.

Her knight in shining armor dumped her shortly after returning to town, but a spiritual soul tie had been formed. Sleeping with Brent knit their souls together.

Brent graduated and joined the Army, leaving her heartbroken and alone.

$\sim$

PAST (TEEN PREGNANCY 1978)

TAMARA CONTINUED HER DESPERATE SEARCH FOR LOVE. SHE MET Luke at a party and fell for him fast.

The party at Luke's house in the next town was in full swing. He was older than Tamara and her friends. He was cool, handsome and mysterious.

"Hey Beautiful, I haven't seen you before." Luke grinned, pressing a beer into her hand.

"Thanks!" she said with a rush of adrenaline.

Luke and Tamara talked into the wee hours of the morning, as partiers passed out on couches, or retreated to bedrooms. The attention he gave her was intoxicating. It went further than the alcohol, and touched the deep longing in her soul to be adored.

Tamara stayed the night in his arms. She woke up and spent hours scrubbing his house, working her fingers to the bone. Maybe Luke would see her value, perhaps even love her one day.

After a few months of hanging out, Tamara was pregnant, and Luke wanted nothing to do with her or their child.

Luke refused her calls when she went into labor.

Tamara gave birth to a perfect, beautiful brown eyed boy. She felt confident that if Luke saw him, he would want to get back together and be a family.

He refused her calls even after Brandon's birth.

Three days after leaving the hospital, Tamara bundled up her precious son and drove to Luke's house.

His new girlfriend opened the door.

"I'm here to see Luke." Tamara said.

With a smirk, she led Tamara into the living room where Luke sat watching a Football game and swigging a beer.

"Sorry to show up unannounced, but since you refuse to answer my calls, you left me no choice." Tamara said apologetically. "You need to meet your son. His name is Brandon Allen."

Luke sat up on the couch as Tamara handed his son to him.

"Does he have all of his toes?" Luke laughed, winking at his girlfriend.

"Of course he does, he is perfect!" Tamara stammered, removing Brandon's booties.

Luke examined his son and handed him back promptly. "What do you want from me Tamara? I'm laid off work right now and don't have any money."

"Nothing, Luke." She said, fighting back tears. "I just thought you would want to meet your only son."

"You gave him my middle name, but I am not even sure if he is mine." Luke's words stung.

"You know he is yours! I have not been with anyone since you, and besides, your mom showed me your baby picture. He looks exactly like you!"

Tamara's hands shook as she fumbled, putting Brandon back into his car seat. Driving away from the house, she sobbed as she spoke to her newborn son, "Jesus wants you Brandon. He loves you so much!"

A DNA test would prove Brandon was indeed Luke's child.

∼

PAST (BRENT AND TAMARA REUNITED 1980)

· · ·

BRENT RETURNED TO THEIR HOMETOWN SOON AFTER BRANDON'S FIRST birthday. Brent reclaimed the territory he had conquered that fateful evening at the beach, and rekindled his relationship with Tamara.

A few weeks into reuniting, Brent was all but living with Tamara and her son. When her parents wanted to stop by, she made a mad dash around the apartment, removing any evidence of him spending nights there. She wanted to make them proud. She wanted to be a respectable Christian woman. She did not know how to stop the cycle of giving herself away to keep a man.

Brent's explosive jealousy soon manifested, as he demanded an accounting of every move Tamara made. If she was home late from being at a friend's, Brent raged and punched walls, accusing her of seeing another man.

Tamara believed that his jealousy showed how much he loved her and wanted her for himself. She was flattered that a man would want to fight over her and for her! She fell in love with him, and wanted to be with him no matter what she had to endure.

"Brent, I'm pregnant." Tamara cried.

"What the hell?" Brent snapped. "I thought you were on the pill!"

"I am, I must have missed a day. I don't know what to do Brent! I can't have another child outside of marriage, it will kill my parents!"

"I am in no way ready to have a child Tamara, I just got a job!"

"I realize that Brent, but what do we do? I don't believe in abortion, Brandon's dad tried to get me to abort him, and there was no way I could go through with it, I can't imagine not having Brandon!"

"Well, I'm not ready for marriage, so we can't have this baby." he coldly replied, grabbing his jacket.

"Where are you going?"

"I need some air." He said, brushing her away.

"Brent!" she cried, throwing her arms back around him. "You can't just leave me! I don't know what to do! I love you! And I want our baby!"

"It's not even a baby yet. It's too early. I'll make the appointment, if that will make it easier for you."

Tamara drew back, searching for any sign of compassion on the man. There was none. "Brent, I can't kill our baby."

"I love you Tamara, but if you don't go through with the abortion, we're done."

"Brent, please! Give me more time!" She pleaded.

Tamara was tormented as Brent refused to answer her calls. If she denied his request, she would lose him. If she had another illegitimate child, her parents and her church would disown her, and she would be alone, with two children on welfare.

All alone.

Unbearable.

Tamara circled the block a few times before finally parking her car in front of Brent's stepmother's house, where he was staying.

The drapes were drawn shut in the picture window leading up to the front door. She trembled as she knocked, her heart pounded so loudly in her ears that it was surprising she could hear the soft footsteps on the other side of the door.

"Hi Lindy, is Brent here?" Shame blushed across Tamara's cheeks.

"Yeah Tamara, but I'm not sure he will see you. Let me ask him, wait here." Lindy's demeanor was stiff, but Tamara could detect a small amount of pity.

A few minutes later Brent appeared, blurry eyed and disheveled. He was obviously coming off an all-night drinking binge. "What do you want Tamara?"

"Can we talk privately? Go somewhere?" she asked.

"Yeah, I guess, let me take a quick shower and I'll be out."

She waited in the car for what felt like an eternity. When Brent finally got in, she broke. Any resistance to his will was completely gone. She would do anything to get him back.

"Okay Brent, you win. I will do as you ask." She sobbed.

"Oh baby." Brent grinned. He pulled her close. "I already made an appointment for next Wednesday. I knew you would come around. I love you so much."

She felt the sting of his threat to abandon her dissipate as he held her in his arms.

But her conscience ached.

The day that Tamara walked into the Clinic with Brent, she felt absolutely numb. Laying on the table, she recited the Dr.'s words, "It's just like having a pap smear, a little discomfort, but no pain, for *either* of you."

Quick.

Simple.

No complications.

Tamara stared at the ceiling. Surrendering her body came natural to her. Surrendering her child inside did not.

Offering her own soul to her idol Brent was not enough. He was an all-consuming god, and he demanded the life of their firstborn.

"Honey, you did so good, I am so proud of you! Now we can move on." Brent cooed as he helped Tamara into the car.

Thoughts came forth, but words failed her, *Move on? God forgive me! What have I done?*

~

THE EVENING OF HER BETROTHAL HAUNTED HER. IT HAD BEEN A FEW months since terminating the pregnancy, when her parents invited the couple over for a nice dinner on the mountain. Shame and guilt blushed across Tamara's face as she heard her father offer Brent more than a handshake and a cold drink.

After dinner, Victoria sliced up big pieces of her famous chocolate cake, while Tamara started to clear away the supper dishes.

Tamara picked up her father's plate, as he pulled the fork off and waved it at Brent, "You know, our women are the best cooks around. Wait until you taste my wife's cake!"

"Yeah, I love Tamara's cooking." Brent responded.

"Brent, she'd make you a fine wife. I would be honored to call you my son-in-law. I have 5 acres parceled off and would be happy to throw a nice trailer on there for you, Tamara and Brandon. The good Lord wants to Bless you, but He can't do it unless you're married."

Tamara felt like a cow with her calf being auctioned off by a farmer.

She was beyond humiliated.

"Yeah, maybe one day Sam. I promise, I'll think about it." Brent said.

A daughter raising a child on welfare was a poor reflection on Sam and Victoria, who were at this time pillars in the local church.

Brent was a blonde, blue eyed All-American young man, fresh out of the Army; the answer to their dreams of covering the shame of their daughter and illegitimate grandson.

The drive back to her low-income apartment was painfully quiet. She desperately wanted a proposal from Brent; but because he loved her, not because he was being bought off. She knew he wasn't ready to settle down.

The same offer had been given over dinner a year and a half prior, to Brandon's biological father Luke. He turned Sam down flat, telling him the only way he would marry his daughter would be because he loved her, which, he did not. She couldn't even win the love of an addict, but at least Luke was an honest one.

Disgusted, Luke had walked away from the deal.

As they entered Tamara's apartment, she prepared herself for the worst, another rejection. But to her surprise, Brent confessed that he was actually thinking it may be time to start a family.

She stared at him in disbelief.

Wait, What? Three months ago, you were not ready for marriage, for children, our baby! Her thoughts went wild!

"So, Tamara, you wanna get married? We might as well."

"Yes!" she gushed, pushing questions from her mind. She kissed the man who would surely take away her shame by putting a ring on her finger.

Finally, she would be okay.

The three holes in her bedroom door should have snapped her back into reality, but fooling herself in his arms came easy. She had been raised to believe and trust deceivers. Once they were married, his jealousy would surely calm down and God would bless them being together. After all, she was living in sin by sleeping with him, so of course it was bad!

Marriage would change all of that.

TAMARA COULD NOT BELIEVE IT WHEN BRENT PRAYED THE SINNER'S prayer in the Pastor's counseling office. After one meeting with her father, he was ready to surrender to Jesus! She thanked God for the miracle. She, after all, could not marry an unsaved man!

Brent performed well at first, making impressive appearances in social settings. He said all the right things to Tamara, and she explained away his unchanging behavior at home.

How could she expect a baby Christian to walk right?

She would give him time.

Brent wasn't as crafty as Sam with hiding his addictions. Brent loved the bars, drugs and women too much to fully enter the Christian scene.

Tamara grasped at any minuscule sign that her husband was changing, that his conversion was true. Christmas and Easter attendance at church, along with an occasional reference to God were better than nothing.

If she just prayed more, and was a better example...

She must maintain hope!

CHAPTER 9

Do not quench the Spirit and do not treat prophecies with contempt but test them all, hold on to what is good, reject every kind of evil.
~ 1 Thessalonians 5:19-22 NIV

PRESENT 1989

"WE CAN'T GO TO YOUR APARTMENT." TERRI PROCLAIMED.

"But my job! I have to go back to work on Monday!" cried Anthony.

Terri continued her militant tone as she veered off the highway and into a Holiday Inn parking lot, "We have to come up with another plan, or we're all dead!"

Terri then artfully painted the gruesome scene of Brent and Ray murdering all of them at Anthony's apartment in California. The scene Brent had described to Tamara years before now flooded back in technicolor. She couldn't take that chance with her children.

Anthony paid for the motel with his American Express as the girls pulled the car around and unloaded their precious cargo.

Upon settling the kids on beds and cots, they huddled together on the floor just outside of their motel room door.

"I can't handle this," whispered Anthony pushing his hands through tufts of immaculately groomed black hair. "I want to go home!"

Tears spilled down familiar curves on Tamara's face, "What home? There is no safe place! There *is* no home!"

Terri, the strongest personality among them, continued to steer their course. "We will start over somewhere new, where no one knows us!"

AFTER A TUMULTUOUS FEW HOURS OF SLEEP, THEY ALL GOT BACK into the SUV and turned onto the street. While eating breakfast at a nearby pancake house, Tamara felt hopeful as her sister Terri reassured them that God had spoken to her and they were all going to be fine.

"We'll never have to eat less than this." Terri's words were met with raised eyebrows.

"What do you mean?" asked Anthony.

"God is going to give us money, and we will always eat in nicer places than this," said Terri.

Having left everything, and being broke except for Anthony's credit card made them vulnerable to this deception.

A sense of *'Because I gave it all up for God, He is going to make us rich'* crept into their souls.

The kids chattered away excitedly over their pancakes, trying to decide what attraction they were going to ride first at Disneyland.

"Uh... plans have kind of changed kids," said Terri interrupting their banter.

"What?" cried Brandon, throwing his fork down on his plate, "I *knew* this was bogus!"

"No, Brandon" Tamara chimed in, "We *are* going to take you to Disneyland, but it will have to be later."

Brandon, flipping back his chair yelled, "I don't want to hear it!"

Tamara swallowed hard as she watched her son disappear down the hallway leading to the bathroom.

Anthony promptly got up and started for the parking lot, "I'm going out for a cigarette!"

Running from things was second nature to them all, it was how they lived, but with God's help, it would not be how they died.

Back on the road again things were quiet, they retreated into their own private worlds. Suddenly Tamara's startled voice broke the silence, "Where did that knife come from?"

One of Ray's ominous hunting knives was lying, plain as day, on the dashboard of the car.

"That was *not* there before!" cried Terri.

"Oh man, I can't take this anymore!" yelled Anthony, confirming that there was no knife there previously. Once again, they all wondered if they were going insane.

"We have to ditch the Forerunner." Terri said, "Ray will trace us with this vehicle anyway, that knife is another sign that death is following us."

At the next exit, they got off the Highway and headed straight for a bus station. Eight tickets to Texas were purchased. Having no idea where they were ultimately going, they loaded all they had in the world onto the bus, trusting that God would show them each step of the way.

Tamara pressed her forehead against the cloudy bus window and stared out at the vehicles passing them by.

They're all heading somewhere, she thought, *it must be nice, knowing their destinations.*

The next stretch of California was a hot and lifeless desert, *exactly* how she felt.

CHAPTER 10

For certain individuals whose condemnation was written about long ago have secretly slipped in among you. They are ungodly people, who pervert the grace of our God into a license for immorality and deny Jesus Christ our only Sovereign and LORD. ~Jude 1:4 NIV

Tamara shifted in her seat, her arm tingling from falling asleep, she'd been in the same position too long. The heat from the window burned hot upon her face, reminding her of that sweltering summer afternoon in her home on the mountain. It was to be an afternoon that would shatter their world forever.

Past (Sam exposed 1987)

In the middle of an intense inner healing prayer led by their mother, Victoria sat back, looking strangely sad at her daughter

Terri and asked, "When was the first time that you said 'No Daddy?'"

The cry that came next was soul piercing as Terri responded in agony, "He raped me!"

The following moments were surreal. Tamara watched the exchange between her mother and sister in horror.

"God, take this rock of hate from my heart!" screamed Victoria, as she thrust her fist upwards, piercing the heavens. Weeping and praying, they clung to one another.

The afternoon and misery seemed endless, but the next day somehow came and they called a family meeting, initially *without* Sam. The lynching mob was formed at their oldest sister Becky's apartment.

A BLANKET OF DARKNESS SETTLED IN ON THEM AS THE DISCUSSION grew volatile. "I'll kill the S.O.B!" yelled Terri's husband Ray, ignoring the fact that he himself was an abuser. Make-up covered the multiple scars on Terri's face from a fit of jealously when he'd hurled a leaded glass at her.

Tamara was beginning to realize that abusers themselves were the ones who wielded the largest sticks in the mob. Her heart felt as if it would burst as she took it all in, knowing the history of the family with all of its glorious sin, including her own, knowing that they all were proclaiming Christ as their Lord, but were now ready to burn their father at the stake.

Tamara felt like a cyclone had landed in the middle of her sister's apartment, picking up debris from every direction; hatred, sadness, grief and rage, and it began to engulf her. It was a destroying wind, not willing that any grace survive in its path.

But didn't Christ say that He had come that we should have life more abundantly? Her distraught thoughts questioned everything.

In her search for the truth of God, confusion overtook her. The more she cried out to know Him, the more her world flew apart! She did not understand that once the light of the true Christ switched on it exposed things that darkness had covered for generations.

"Not one of you is any more righteous than my father!" Tamara screamed over the commotion, knowing full well they would turn on her.

In fact, she felt betrayal within herself for not joining the hatred on her sister's behalf. She agonized for Terri but felt she could be healed, while her father was headed for Hell.

Victoria swung around to her daughter, eyes flashing, "Don't you dare measure me against that trash!"

All Tamara could think of was how Christ had saved her from her own sins, even aborting a child. It was crucial to forgive or they would not be forgiven. She had been the recipient of such amazing mercy and grace that had triumphed over judgement, and now she was ready to demonstrate that toward her father.

Was it too soon?

What exactly was the waiting period to offer mercy and grace?

Her eyes ached to see all people redeemed from the curse, walking in their true identity free of the sin that warped and shaped them into disfigured creatures.

"Aren't we supposed to be Christians?" Drawing in a deep breath, Tamara continued, "We all have sin! We need to pray for him to repent and be truly saved!"

The crowd disbursed, angrily mumbling. Perhaps Tamara's words hit like the time Jesus challenged a crowd in the New Testament, asking who wanted to be first to stone the adulteress. Stones clacked together in their pockets, as they headed for the door.

CHAPTER 11

I wrote to you in my letter not to associate with sexually immoral
people- not at all meaning the people of this world who are
immoral, or the greedy and swindlers, or idolaters. In that case you
would have to leave this world. But now I am writing to you that you
must not associate with anyone who claims to be a brother or sister
but is sexually immoral or greedy, an idolater or slanderer, a
drunkard or swindler. Do not even eat with such people.
~1 Corinthians 5:9-11 NIV

PAST (TAMARA REACHES OUT TO SAM 1987)

NONE OF THE IMMEDIATE FAMILY WOULD SPEAK TO SAM AFTER THE
meeting at Becky's apartment. Victoria moved out of their
mountain home and stayed at Terri's.

Tamara believed that her father was guilty, but she did not
believe that he was beyond redemption. She wanted to show him

the true unconditional love of Christ, the love that had saved her.
She would reach out to him, even if she had to go alone.

Tamara tended Sam for a few weeks, speaking veiled truths to
coax him into repentance. She truly felt she was reaching him, that
God's kindness through her would break him. He would come
clean, admit to his sin, and be saved. The family unit would be
whole.

The true extent of her Father's hardness of heart came out over
coffee and dessert, the night of his birthday.

Savoring his final bite of chocolate cake, Sam sat his coffee cup
down and leaned intimately into Tamara, patted her hand and with
the gentlest voice said, "Now you know that I could never have done
those awful things your sister said."

Tamara felt her face flush, feeling foolish. He was playing upon
her affections.

The truth came rushing in.

He was toying with her, and had no intention of ever repenting.
He wanted Tamara to cover his sin, just as Victoria had done for so
many years.

As she saw her father to the door, he hugged her goodbye and
his body shook with the embrace. Something that would have
usually called forth emotion from her, but did not.

Tamara sensed it was empty, a dead man's hug.

As she closed her front door, she shuddered, knowing that God
was closing another.

To stand with him now, you will be comforting his way to Hell. She knew
what God was whispering into her Spirit.

She must step aside and let God deal with him. For the first time
Tamara had an understanding of the Scripture (she had always felt
too harsh) in 1st Corinthians 5:11, that said not to even eat with *such
a one.*

CHAPTER 12

But as for you, the LORD took you and brought you out of the iron-smelting furnace, out of Egypt, to be the people of his inheritance, as you now are. ~Deuteronomy 4:20 NIV

Present 1989

In an obscure little town, they disembarked from the bus and found out their luggage would not be in until the next morning.

Hot, tired and hungry, they went to a nearby motel and tucked in. The kids were bouncing off the walls and beds, still bewildered by their trip to nowhere in particular, yet excited, as kids are for an adventure.

Each evening, as they traveled farther from their homes, the kids shared a bit more of what Daddies did while Mommies were away. Much like a newborn who can only see distorted images until their eyes mature and things are sharpened, the children had their vision warped.

Their oppressors worked in tandem with dark entities, keeping them from sharing what was being done. Though seeing, they were told they did not see.

What was sickening normal life to them would take years to undo, but first, they must be safe.

Terri and Tamara continually reassured the children they were starting over and would not have to see their fathers again. In the safety of their mother's words, they divulged more information.

Alicia told a detailed account of what her father had made her do one afternoon after he got out of the shower. It was almost more than they could bear to hear. The incest they had grown up with was happening in their very own homes!

They knew all along that their husbands were drunkards, drug addicts, womanizers, physically and emotionally abusive, but they had no idea of the sexual abuse their children had suffered. Tamara herself was beaten early on in the marriage, but that eventually stopped once she recommitted her life to Christ. She pleaded with Brent to go easier on the boys with discipline, but she had never seen blood drawn, so in her mind it wasn't abuse.

To compare her childhood upbringing with theirs would never be a healthy measuring stick. Only by renewing her mind by the Word of God, and listening to the Holy Spirit, would she learn how to parent.

Once she surrendered fully to Christ, she truly believed Brent too, would change. He would be a great father and husband one day. If she simply prayed harder, and more often, someday all would be fine. She'd heard many testimonies and Victoria's prophecies always confirmed that the men were coming to God. Their family would be healed.

Thoughts of suicide plagued her as she overheard conversations among the children. Grueling hours went on, as they called them one by one into the hall to let them share about anyone who had hurt them prior to the trip. Tamara could see the uncomfortable struggle in each child. Terri's oldest daughter Alicia's account would surely mean a prison sentence for Ray.

Tamara's youngest son Joshua shared about taking a nap with

his father. Her son's description of what Daddy did, made her cringe. It was foreplay he often did with her. He had not completed his dastardly deed, but Tamara was certain that without God's intervention, it would only have been a matter of time. God indeed drew a line in the sand, as their exodus off the mountain was only a week after that particular naptime.

Tamara distinctly recalled Joshua throwing a screaming fit as she lay him down that day to take a nap with his Dad. When Brent worked the graveyard shift, he always insisted that the younger boys take a nap with him because he missed them so much. Tamara was baffled as to why her son was throwing such a fit because it was their normal routine. Now, looking back, she wanted to vomit.

How could she not have known?

How could she have let her children go through that?

Oh Lord, you know that I just thought Joshua was tired and not wanting to sleep, I had no idea! I would have never knowingly put him in harm's way!

Her thoughts and prayers collided. She felt no relief, only despair at what a horrible mother she had been.

The kids inadvertently continued to reveal things as they played around, teasing and punching one another, taunting each other with prodding questions.

The adults now saw life events remembered through the children's eyes, and what was once hidden, now became glaringly obvious and terrifying.

To go on was almost more than she could bear, but she knew that if she didn't survive, her sons would go back to their abusive father. Suicide would be selfish. It would be about her. She must choose to live despite the horrendous guilt.

Long after the kids were asleep, Tamara and her siblings, rightly devastated, went back to their knees in prayer. They had often wondered if leaving like they did was too drastic. Yet upon further revelations, they knew God had allowed this crazy trip to bring them out of deception. They now understood that the children would have never revealed what happened if they were in the same town as their perpetrators.

The children had asked many times if they would see their father's again, and were reassured that they would not.

Tamara and Terri never intended on going back.

CHAPTER 13

THE ENEMY BOASTED, 'I WILL PURSUE, I WILL OVERTAKE THEM. I will divide the spoils; I will gorge myself on them. I will draw my sword and my hand will destroy them. ~Exodus 15:9 NIV

PRESENT 1989

TAMARA AND TERRI WERE AWAKENED FROM THEIR EXHAUSTED slumber by a blow so fierce it felt it would cut them in half. They had simultaneously been thrown upright in the Queen bed they shared. A menacing force struck them with a dull edged sword, but as their eyes scanned the dimly lit room, nothing was there. *Something* did not want them free. They had broken out of hell itself, but were being pursued by an invisible demonic realm.

One could almost hear the commission "If they won't come back willingly under deception, kill them!"

"What happened?" Anthony yelled from across the room.

"Something tried to kill us!" Tamara cried.

More cries for mercy ascended to God's throne. Only by a

miracle did the children get back to sleep despite the insanity of that night.

The next morning, hands shaking from lack of sleep and trauma, Tamara had a hard time putting in her contacts. She didn't have her eye solution, as her bag was on a bus somewhere, so she had to soak them in water. Her eyes burned from exhaustion and crying.

The pain for her children burned more.

Only the hope of Christ giving them a new life would propel her forward.

Terri had pointed out to her that their own mother could not help them process their pain because she had never processed her own. Tamara made a conscious decision to face the pain, and knew she would have to continually make it, again and again.

As soon as the troops awakened and ate their continental breakfast, they all headed for the bus station.

Tamara and Terri, both accustomed to never leaving the house without dressing to the nines, now sported rumpled clothing, flat hair, and puffy eyes painted with drab shades of sorrow. As they made their way onto the bus, they noticed how differently they were treated. Only the day before they had experienced people smiling and moving aside for them, sharing seats.

Today, people ignored, glared or pushed them. Hitting bottom was a long fall, and they hit hard.

Their missing luggage was at the next station, they loaded it into the rental car and hit the road.

TAMARA WAS A LONG WAY FROM THE RESPECTFUL LIFE IN HER hometown. She had worked so hard to change and become a godly woman. Where Tamara and her sister had at one time taught Bible studies and been honored, they were now the gossip of the marketplace.

Anthony was not used to living on faith, and catching grimy

busses. His job afforded him the luxury of flying first class around the world on a whim.

While the women ran for their lives and the lives of their children, their small town was abuzz with rumors. It was said that they had gone out to sacrifice their children in the wilderness. The only altar Tamara put her children on was *God's*, for His deliverance and protection.

CHAPTER 14

Lord, you alone are my inheritance, my cup of blessing. You guard
all that is mine
. ~Psalm 16:5 NL

PRESENT 1989

"THE CREDIT CARD WON'T WORK," ANTHONY REPORTED AS HE
walked out of the Mini-Mart towards the car.

"What do you mean it won't work? It has to!" Terri panicked.

Anthony needed a cigarette, badly and they had no cash. His
credit card and their faith were all they had to get them closer to a
new life. The cash that Tamara had brought was long gone and she
had destroyed her bank card before leaving her hometown. She
believed that Anthony's California apartment was their final
destination.

"I tried it and it was declined." Anthony repeated as he bent down and picked up a stained and weathered cigarette lying in front of the car.

Lighting up, he inhaled deeply, as if taking in a long-lost friend, and turned to his sisters, "I talked to a credit card representative and they told me that I can't use my card anymore until I make a payment."

"I can't believe you are smoking that!" said Tamara in disgust.

Terri quickly changed the subject back to their dire position, "We're just going to have to go back to the motel room and pray."

While the kids jumped on the beds, the three of them gathered in the hallway and prayed.

"Anthony," Terri's commanding voice broke their petitioning of heaven. "That card is not yours, it is God's. He signed it. You need to stop worrying about it and continue to pay for everything with it."

"But it won't work!" said Anthony.

"Yes, it will," said Terri. "I saw God's signature on your card, it is no longer yours!"

And it *did*, for every other provision they needed, for the rest of their journey. Once again confusion swirled within Tamara's soul, as she saw the provision, but the voice that proclaimed it was dark. Tamara had lived in fear so long that everything was processed through it. She feared the devil and feared God. When anyone in prayer started a sentence with "God said," her allegiance followed. She was trained to never question authority. The perfect set-up for a cult. Tamara left the cult, but the teachings still entangled her.

Tamara *knew* that God *alone* was her provider, her inheritance. Her only security lay within that truth, one she had proclaimed before she left the family mountain…

∼

PAST (ONE MONTH PRIOR TO THE TRIP OFF THE MOUNTAIN 1989)

VICTORIA STOPPED BY TAMARA'S HOUSE ON THE MOUNTAIN, READY

for battle. "You are pulling away from me Tamara, you and your sister are hurting me!" Victoria wept, pushing away the tea mug her daughter handed her.

Tamara had pleaded on her knees to the Lord countless times for her mother to come back from the brink of insanity. God had given her gracious words to share with her mother, but each time Victoria refused to repent and became harder, pointing out everyone's sin but her own.

This day was no different and Tamara, exhausted from fighting deception and sin in her own life, did not want to fight her mother.

"Mom, we love you but you won't take Dad off the throne. He is an evil dictator and the Hell continues. Nothing is changing for the better, no matter how much we pray. This isn't the abundant life Jesus promised!" she cried.

Victoria pridefully snapped at her daughter, "So, you think you don't have idols?"

"Of course I do, but I am repenting and trying to keep God first!" Tamara promptly got up from the kitchen table, grabbed her purse and headed to the door.

Victoria followed on her daughter's heels shouting, "You have no inheritance from me!"

Great sadness took precedence over rejection in Tamara's heart. All she could think as she drove away was, *that's okay, all I want is Jesus for my inheritance.*

CHAPTER 15

DEAR FRIENDS, DO NOT BELIEVE EVERY SPIRIT, BUT TEST THE SPIRITS to see whether they are from God, because many false prophets have gone out into the world. ~1 John 4:1 NIV

PRESENT 1989

"YOU'VE GOT TO THROW THOSE OUT!" TERRI BARKED AT HER sister.

"My writings?" Tamara asked in shock.

"Yes, you've got to let them go, they've become too important to you."

Tamara surveyed the journals spread out on the floor in front of her, "But these writings are my heart, all the times Jesus talked to me, and poems that God has given me over the past few years."

Much like her mother Victoria, Terri made Tamara feel like a spiritual gnat, swatting her away from her own stand on any given issue.

"You've dragged them with us long enough, God is asking you if you trust Him to let go of them." said Terri.

Tamara wanted desperately to please the Lord. But, did He really ask that of her? She feared challenging Terri's question. She could not take a chance on disobeying God's voice.

In case it was.

Tamara obediently took her bag of journals and tossed them into the dumpster.

The cassette player and Christian worship tapes Tamara brought on the trip were another of her most prized possessions. The music took her to a secret place, where nothing could touch her. She lay on her bed with her eyes closed, listening intently, trying her best to settle her anxious soul, when Terri plopped on the corner of the bed. "You know that music is tainted with the world Tamara."

"What? No!" Tamara leaned up on one elbow.

"Yes, Tamara, God showed me that He wants news songs written. If you look deep in your heart, you will know that there is something wrong with the worship leaders, it's about their own glory. And, there's something else I need to tell you. Remember that conference I went to with mom in Canada?"

"Yeah." said Tamara.

"Well, I never told you what happened the last day of the conference. Mom invited several ladies to come back to our motel room to pray. She made me lie down on a bed next to one woman who had been through a Satanic ritual, to go through the deliverance with her. I was to stand in the gap for her, like Jesus. I didn't want to Tamara, but I couldn't say no!" Terri began to cry.

"Oh my gosh Terri, what happened!" Tamara sat up and put her arm around her sister as she continued the story.

"Mom prayed in her language, you know, her warfare tongue. It got loud and intense, and suddenly I felt like I was on a cold cement slab. I saw a horrible mask over me, and my hands became distorted and paralyzed. The pain became so unbearable, I begged mom to make it stop but she wouldn't! She said I had to be willing to even die for that woman!" Terri sobbed.

"No! I can't believe mom made you do that in the name of the Lord! That is not our Jesus!"

Terri blew her nose into the tissue her sister handed her. "No, it wasn't. Isn't. And I will never let her or anyone control me, ever again!"

Tamara nodded in agreement but was perplexed at Terri's next demand.

"You need to throw out your music tapes, tonight! They can't even be in our room!"

"But Terri, I learned to worship God with them, that music is not tainted, it is Holy!"

"Tamara, you need to listen to me, God is bringing new songs on the earth. He is throwing out the old. He wants all things new!"

There it was.

A little sprinkling of Scripture. God was wanting to make things new.

The rest of the evening Terri spent convincing Tamara of this new revelation.

Compassion for her sister and blind loyalty was all that was needed for the manipulation to control Tamara. She had been raised to follow her parents without question and she quickly transferred her submission to her sister since her parents were out of the picture. Tamara loaded up her collection of music and walked them out to the Dumpster.

CHAPTER 16

Although you wash yourself with soap and use an abundance of cleansing powder, the stain of your guilt is still before me," declares the Sovereign LORD. "How can you say, 'I am not defiled; I have not run after the Baals'? See how you behaved in the valley; consider what you have done. You are a swift she-camel running here and there. ~ Jeremiah 2:22-23 NIV

PAST (ENTER JEZEBEL 1986)

TAMARA'S MOM, AN EAGER STUDENT IN THE SPIRITUAL REALM, shared what she learned with Tamara.

"Sometimes I sit on your dad's lap and talk with the demons in him. I have gotten a lot of insight into the demonic realm from them!"

"But Mom!" Tamara cried, "They're liars, they won't tell you the truth! Why would you even want to talk to them!"

Victoria smugly replied, "I have a deeper understanding than you, Tamara."

As Tamara immersed herself in the Bible for truth, the scriptures showed her another world at play. In the book of Revelations, she'd read about Jezebel, a wicked queen of the Old Testament who was the embodiment of a rebellious evil spirit. The text spoke of people that held to Jezebel's teachings claiming to know the deep things of Satan.

The red flags were flying for some time, but Tamara continually dismissed them, as she admired her mother and wanted to believe that her motives were pure.

During another prayer session, Victoria confessed another incident that opened her up to this demonic presence. "Do you kids remember that big party we had at my house, when I excused myself to go lay down because I was coming down with a migraine?"

"Yeah. I remember." Replied Tamara.

"Well, as I lay on my bed, I rehearsed all of the hell we were going through and I got more and more angry. God seemed so distant and powerless. Then I thought about Jesus' words, "No one can serve two masters. Either you will hate the one and love the other, or you will be devoted to the one and despise the other. You cannot serve both God and money." Matthew 6:24 (NIV)

Victoria pursed her lips as she continued, "I was so angry, and I wondered, 'Why can't I serve two masters?'"

She went on to share how when she had returned to the party, she felt strange, and was met with bewildered expressions on people's faces. "People said I looked ashen, but I actually felt much better. The headache was gone and I felt more powerful and more in control of my life. God has shown me that it was then a Jezebel spirit entered my body."

"Oh Mom!" Tamara kneeled in front of her mother. "Let's pray now, you can be delivered from that foul spirit!"

"No worries Tamara." Victoria grinned. "I already asked forgiveness and I am free of her."

VICTORIA HAD QUITE A FOLLOWING AS SHE BECAME PROFICIENT AT prophesying over people's lives. People became enamored.

Tamara was the one enlisted to keep her mother busy and away from the mountain home all morning. When it was finally time, Tamara drove her mother up the long driveway. Victoria's mouth dropped open as she saw car after car parked all over her property and a huge "Victoria Day" banner that hung across white pillars on front of their Southern plantation style home.

Tamara guided her weeping mother through the sea of ladies surrounding her. *Oh Lord,* Tamara prayed, *how special my mother is, she touches so many women for you. Bless her Lord!*

One by one women shared how Victoria had impacted their lives through prophecy, and showered her with gifts.

Tamara chided herself for judging her mother. After all, nobody was perfect. Working with her mother behind the scenes, witnessing the backbiting and control, did not seem to stop her ministry. *Victoria must be okay*, she thought. It was her own heart that needed work!

Victoria was initially received by the Pastors at different churches they would visit, but they eventually cut off all communication with her.

"You know why they don't like me don't you Tamara?"

"No, Mom, why?"

"It's because I see through them, and they know it. God shows me their sin, and they don't like it! I have been commissioned to bring correction to them."

Tamara wanted to believe her mother's repentance had been real, but sadly continued to witness the controlling ways of Jezebel, all in the name of God.

Everywhere Victoria went, mayhem soon followed.

Didn't Jesus say that signs and wonders would follow believers?

THE CLOSER TAMARA PRESSED IN TO KNOW GOD, THE DEEPER Brent went into using drugs and alcohol.

Tamara was awakened at midnight with an almost audible voice, "Bind the spirit of Jezebel over your husband!"

Tamara immediately obeyed the Lord, and crawled out of bed. Pulling on her robe, she went and grabbed her Bible. Brent had gone out drinking, and she knew he would not be home until after the bars closed. Tamara no longer retaliated by doing the same since becoming Spirit-filled. She knew that the only thing fruitful was to intercede in the moments of gut twisting pain.

Brent stormed through the door at three a.m. "I've met someone, she is even more beautiful than you are, you are out, she is in!"

Tamara continued her fervent prayers for protection. The children had spent the night at their grandparents, so while Brent went into the kitchen to forage for something to eat, she slipped into Brandon's room to continue praying.

"Where did you go? I will find you!" Brent bellowed from their bedroom.

Tamara remained quiet as she asked God what to do next. Before she could do anything, Brent burst into Brandon's bedroom. He walked over to the bunkbeds and threw the covers back, "Do you think you can hide from me? When I get ahold of you, you will be sorry!"

Tamara was praying, sitting in the window seat adjacent to the bunkbeds. She froze, knowing in his drunken and drugged rage, he could kill her.

Turning around from the bunkbeds, he scanned the room, looking directly at Tamara, and left. She heard the front door open and him yelling, "Where are you!"

Tamara was in awe. She knew that God had made her invisible to Brent!

She opened the window and pushed the screen out, and ran for her life down the road to her mother's house.

Tamara called 911 once she got safely inside her mother's home. After an hour or so, the police came and told her that Brent was very sorry and calm now, he just wanted his wife home. As usual, no arrest was made.

The next day Tamara talked to Brent's sister, who was her best friend. "Amber, Brent isn't getting better, he is getting worse! Last night he told me he'd met someone and that I was out, she was in!"

"Yeah, I know who is it Tamara, it is the girl from Mini-Mart. Someone saw them dancing together at the Chinese restaurant last night."

Upon further investigation, Tamara found out that the girl was dancing and kissing Brent, but suddenly, she walked off the dance floor after realizing he was a married man. The time that she did? Midnight.

A few months later Tamara found out that the beautiful girl Brent spoke of, had Aids.

CHAPTER 17

Break the arm of the wicked man; call the evildoer to account for
his wickedness that would not otherwise be found out.
~Psalm 10:15 NIV

PRESENT 1989

CLOSING HER EYES, TAMARA SLID DEEPLY INTO THE MOTEL BATHTUB,
but not deep enough to drown the memories. She relived the
devastation of the first confrontation of her father.

PAST (SAM CONFRONTED 1987)

VICTORIA, HEAD HELD HIGH, LED HER CHILDREN INTO THE COZY
family room where they had laughed, cried, and entertained
countless guests over the years. The beautiful antiques and quaint

paintings warmed the room with a false sense of well-being. They had all been in much prayer but Tamara could clearly see that her mother had no peace.

"Your daughter has something to say to you!" Victoria barked sharply at Sam.

Sam sat forward, shifting his focus toward Terri, "You have something to say to me?" He asked in that tone that put the fear of God in Tamara since childhood.

"Dad, you know what you did to me!" Terri's words tumbled out like rocks falling from a cave she had been buried in for years.

"I didn't do *anything* to you." He responded in a low growl.

Sam sat wringing his hands, his glare deepening and jaw twitching.

All in the room sat sickeningly silent, frozen with fear. Their very breath was captive.

Terri's tortured voice broke the silence, "Dad, you know you raped me!"

"That's a filthy lie!" Sam's face contorted with rage.

Victoria leapt from the couch, "And how about your affair with the neighbor, do you want to tell us about that too?"

In a prior prayer session, Anthony confessed that when he was small, Sam drove him into town. While passing the neighbor's house Sam made a comment on how beautiful the neighbor was. Further down the road they passed a car parked in a wooded area on a little dirt path. Sam turned to Anthony and said, "That's how people meet to have affairs, they park their cars where no one will notice, and leave in one car together."

Victoria was convinced that Sam had had an affair with the neighbor.

Even amidst the turmoil, Tamara was perplexed, it seemed her mother was more outraged at the thought of an affair with another woman than her own daughter's molestation!

Victoria moved toward the door screaming profanity, vowing to see him rot in prison. Sam lunged for her purse to prevent her from leaving. She held tightly to it, hysterically slugging him.

Tamara could not believe her eyes, this man who had ruled over them, their entire lives with an iron fist, was now a weak old man, without the strength to wrestle a purse away from a woman.

A verse came alive to her, when Satan fell from heaven.

THOSE WHO SEE YOU WILL GAZE AT YOU, SAYING, "IS THIS THE MAN who made the earth tremble, who shook kingdoms...?" Isaiah 14:16 (NASB)

FROM CHILDHOOD TO THAT DAY, TAMARA HAD TREMBLED IN HER father's satanic presence. This day, that changed.

His rule thrown down. She saw her father powerless to do any more harm to her. She was no longer his captive, a stronger man had entered her father's house, The Lord Jesus Christ. He *was* her home now.

Tamara and Terri were baffled that Sam would rather sit alone in that big house, losing his family, than admit to his sin.

Tamara wanted his confession so they could forgive and be restored. In her mind, if he apologized, it would go no further, no police, no separation, just counseling and reconciliation.

With all that Tamara was, she believed the Good News, that Christ came to make dead men alive, turn monsters into saints, and nightmares into dreams.

CHAPTER 18

If they had been thinking of the country they had left, they would
have had opportunity to return. Instead, they were longing for a
better country-a heavenly one. Therefore, God is not ashamed to be
called their God, for he has prepared a city for them.
~Hebrews 11:15-16 NIV

PRESENT 1989

TEXAS TURNED OUT TO BE JUST ANOTHER STOPOVER, WITH ANOTHER
motel, more prayer and unanswerable questions from the children.

"God gave me a phone number" Terri said. "We are supposed
to call this man for help. He is going to give us money."

"Are you serious?" asked Tamara.

"Yes," Terri replied as she lifted the phone off its cradle.

"Hi, you don't know me, but you are supposed to help us." Terri
said to the man on the other end of the line. The man inquired how
she had gotten his private number.

"God gave it to me." Terri responded.

After a few minutes of explaining their plight, she abruptly hung up. She told Anthony and Tamara that he refused to listen to God and would not give them money. She explained that he was shady, and used his private line for illicit purposes, and she had exposed him.

They had all run from Victoria's influences, her mind reading, fortune telling and other forms of witchcraft. Tamara shuddered as she lay back on the bed, looking at her sister, bewildered by the similarities…*but she has so much wisdom, and knowledge of the Scriptures,* her thoughts guided her away from the obvious.

Tamara once again chose to ignore the glaring checks in her own spirit.

Falling asleep was something she longed for to escape, but inevitably, Tamara slipped back into a scene of her past. She remembered the time when Victoria left Sam upon revelation of Terri's abuse.

THE SNOWY DRIVEWAY THAT LED TO HER PARENT'S MOUNTAIN HOME was deafeningly silent, the usual crunch of the wheels biting into the ice encrusted snow, eerily absent.

Tamara's breathing slowed as she made her way up to the front entrance of the family fortress. Her body shook from the penetrating cold, even with the heat blasted on high. She did not want to take her mother back to that wicked place, but Victoria insisted she must retrieve some things that night.

Moments before turning onto the cement parking pad, a loud thud rocked the SUV. Some kind of creature landed on top of the vehicle, and they began to slide down the edge of the driveway. Claws gripped the rooftop, forcing it to tumble into the field below.

"*Mom!*" screamed Tamara as she looked over at her mother, "*Mom! Pray!* A demonic creature has us! Please Mom! Pray! Get it off!"

To Tamara's horror, her mother stared blankly ahead as if in a trance. Tamara called on the name of Jesus and commanded the demon to let go. Instantly the SUV quit sliding.

~

Joshua's screams ripped Tamara out of slumbering memory and into the present. It was to remain a pattern, the crisis at hand continually kept her from processing the crisis of the past.

Joshua awoke with an excruciating earache. She must tend her son and unpack the events of the night terrors later. Having come into a new town, they had no idea where an all-night pharmacy was to purchase medicine. Tamara lay next to her sobbing son, praying fervently for him to be healed and for the surrounding motel guests not to call the front desk...or the police.

God brought to mind a vial of anointing oil she always carried with her. She ran it under warm water, and poured it into her sons' ear, calling on the Great Physician Jesus to heal him. Within moments he quietly went to sleep. Tamara lay down beside him, worshiping God. She heard that warm oil was a temporary fix, but this was not temporary. Joshua never did have another problem with his ear.

They all believed this was a sign. God was going to take care of them.

CHAPTER 19

For to us a child is born, to us a son is given, and the government will be on his shoulders. He will be called Wonderful Counselor, Mighty God, Everlasting Father, Prince of Peace. ~Isaiah 9:6 NIV

ANTHONY SPRAWLED OUT ACROSS THE HOTEL BED IN THE MIDDLE OF where the girls sat, and interrupted their conversation. "Let's get all dressed up and go out to a nice dinner."

The children excitedly grabbed their coats and lined up at the door. Tamara changed into a dress in the bathroom, but then laid back down on the bed.

"You guys go on ahead without me," Tamara said, shading her eyes from the lamp. She was fine one moment and then, *wham*, without a hint of warning, a migraine, like nothing she'd ever known, was upon her.

After everyone left, she crawled into the bathroom, hoping a hot bath might help. The warm water rushed in on her head and she begged God to make the pain stop. She wanted to vomit but feared her head might explode with the effort.

The emotions were more than her body could bear. The events that had taken place no longer hung back, but crowded to the forefront of her soul, demanding attention. The abuse of her children and nieces was a tipping point, teetering towards an abyss of despair, or falling headlong into the hope of a redeeming Savior.

When her family returned, she was still achy, but the onslaught had subsided. Plopping onto the bed beside Tamara, Terri whispered into her sister's ear; "You had that headache because you're suppressing the truth about your own sexual abuse."

"What?" Tamara asked.

Anthony turned a show on for the kids and dropped to his knees, elbows on the bed, salivating for a morsel of gossip.

"But Mom said that Dad never touched me, that I wouldn't have survived it." said Tamara.

"Yeah, well, she was wrong, I know Dad did something to you too!" said Terri.

Tamara rolled over, facing the opposite direction of her siblings piercing stares. "I don't think so, I have no memories. Besides, I was the ugly one that he rejected, remember?"

Terri, rose from the bed and retorted, "Well, I know he did!"

OVER THEIR MORNING RITUAL OF PASTRIES AND COFFEE FROM THE lobby, Tamara shared with her siblings, "You guys, I had a dream that we stayed the night with Oprah Winfrey!"

Terri and Anthony laughed, but she went on, "It was *so* real. We were all sitting around on big overstuffed couches talking, and Oprah had on white silk pajamas!"

Before long the dream was interpreted by the trio as the next step in their journey. They were to go to Chicago and ask Oprah for help!

They had seen her reunite families on television and confront abusers, she would surely understand! The next day they purchased train tickets and were on their way to the Windy City.

UPON ARRIVING IN CHICAGO, THEY RENTED A CAR AND CRUISED THE streets looking for Oprah's Studio.

"There it is!" cried Anthony, pointing across the street.

They pulled into a parking lot and while Anthony stayed in the car with the kids, Tamara and Terri approached the building.

They talked to a nice receptionist who informed them that Oprah was on vacation and the studio was closed for two weeks due to the Holidays.

Once again, their hope for help plummeted. They drove aimlessly through the city on Christmas Eve, festive Christmas lights aglow, holiday music streaming from the radio. The words to familiar old songs they once sang in fun, now haunted them.

Anthony made a decision amongst the gloom to check them into one of the finest hotels in Chicago. "We're going to have a nice Christmas!" he declared.

The children's weary faces lit up as they walked into the lobby, taking in the beautiful surroundings and the biggest Christmas tree they had ever laid eyes on. But what caught their attention most was the gold and glass elevator, bidding them to come and take a ride.

They checked in and after a few trips up and down the elevator, they settled into their room.

"Let's take the kids down to the pool, they need to have some fun." said Anthony

Wholeheartedly agreeing, they all changed into their suits. Down by the pool they watched as their children laughed, splashed and played. A little more hope slipped into Tamara's thoughts, *maybe we can be happy and normal, like this.*

Her thoughts were soon interrupted by her niece Alicia's screams echoing in the pool area. She had cracked her head on the side of the cement wall while jumping into the pool.

Blood gushed down her face and she wriggled and screamed in her mother's arms. Alicia settled down as her mom applied pressure with a towel on her forehead.

Tamara and Anthony coaxed the rest of the children out of their blissful moment of play in the water.

Dismally, they all headed back to the hotel room.

Tamara started to give way to the lie, that all good things were to be cut short.

Each time there was a shred of hope in her heart, it was as if Satan darted through, grabbing it like a purse snatcher, mocking her for believing differently.

She had grown accustomed to trusting in oppression more than God's goodness.

Exactly what Satan had in mind.

Back in their hotel room, Tamara questioned her sister, "Shouldn't we take her to the hospital for stitches?"

"No," snapped Terri, "It's not that bad, we just need to bandage it."

It was after all, Christmas Eve, and they were already paranoid of being taken back to the insanity they had left behind.

However, the reality of not being able to take the kids for medical treatment was chipping away at their illusions of starting over, without first confronting their past.

ANTHONY AND TERRI WENT OUT TO FIND A DRUGSTORE TO GET bandages and ointment for Alicia's head and charge one gift per child. They also hoped to find a tree lot that might accept a credit card; so, when they got back, they could tend Alicia's wound, and all go on a tree hunt.

Every lot they passed greeted them with a "Closed" sign.

Not a tree anywhere.

Finally, at the last lot Terri spotted a single branch on the ground.

Anthony jumped out, laid down on the snow and extended his arm beneath the chained fence gate, the branch was barely within his reach.

So grateful for the humble offering from this cold city, they went back to their hotel.

The ice bucket in their room served as a tree stand and they handcrafted toilet paper into neat little bows that adorned their Christmas branch. Charlie Brown had nothing on them.

Tamara felt sorry for the children who had always been showered with more gifts than any child needed.

But this Christmas they were *safe*.

She smiled as she took in their pathetic branch, with five crudely wrapped gifts around it. She had no idea where they would go next. But they were out of harm's way and tomorrow was Christmas.

They gathered the kids and sang Christmas carols around their little branch, thanking God for sending His Son to be born in a manger. They needed no lights on their tree, as *they* were the lights shining in the darkness on that cold Chicago evening.

CHAPTER 20

In the shelter of your presence you hide them from all human intrigues; you keep them safe in your dwelling from accusing tongues. ~Psalm 31:20 NIV

TAMARA CLEARLY SAW THE WEIGHT ON HER BROTHER'S SHOULDERS. She knew he wanted to help her and their sister Terri get their children away from their abusive world, but the pull on him was obvious. He wanted to return to life as he knew it.

"I miss Lance. I just want to have a stiff drink and have him hold me. He is probably worried sick about me!" Anthony bemoaned.

"But you broke it off before we even left Anthony, you know that God has better for you. You were not even happy with Lance!" Terri said.

"I know, I know." said Anthony. "I just miss him. I don't know why God doesn't take the desire away!"

The girls had no answers at the ready for their brother, they simply reassured him of God's understanding and that He would not require anything of him, that He would not provide for and walk through with him.

They could quote more scriptures, but he already knew them.

Revelation of them through the Holy Spirit was what he needed.

Over morning coffee and bagels, Anthony shared a dream he had with his sisters. "I had a dream that we were from Newcastle."

"What?" the girls chimed in unison.

"I think God is giving us direction where we are to start over." he said.

"Where in the heck is Newcastle?" Tamara asked.

They pulled out a map and stretched it out on the round table by the window.

"There it is" said Terri, "It's in Pennsylvania."

After a few hours of conversation, Terri told them she understood why they were to go to there. "Kathryn Kuhlman's ministry was based in Pittsburgh. I am to receive her anointing."

The duplicity within Tamara was real. She was one moment in fear of her sister and in the next, in awe of the powerful call on her life. She hoped the anointing would break the chains from the past and Terri would be healed and go forward in ministry.

"We need to go to Pittsburgh then." Tamara complied.

With that, they packed up and left for the airport.

Unbeknownst to them, their father Sam hired a detective who was hot on their trail. Their strange disappearance only supported Sam's innocence and that his poor family had gone over the edge seeking God.

They were now in the Newspaper, "Local Family Missing!"

CHAPTER 21

Woe to you, teachers of the law and Pharisees, you hypocrites! You are like whitewashed tombs, which look beautiful on the outside but on the inside are full of the bones of the dead and everything unclean. ~Matthew 23:27 NIV

Upon deplaning in Pennsylvania, they rented another car and searched for a church, a refuge from the storm. The church buildings stood gray and tall, with no sign of life. Church after church, closed, standing silent before them like whitewashed tombs.

No Oprah, no church, from where would their help come from? Tamara looked upon the darkening sky and a beloved song from the 121st Psalm flooded her soul,

I lift my eyes up unto the Mountains, where does my help come from?
My help comes from you, Maker of Heaven, Creator of the Earth,
Oh, how I need you Lord you are my only hope, you're my only prayer, so I will
wait for you to come and rescue me, come and give me life.

AND SO, ONCE AGAIN, SHE WAITED.

DRIVING ALONG THE WATER, THE NIGHT SKY OFFERED STARS TO light their way, interplaying with the artificial lights from the sprawling architecture. The beauty momentarily brought relief to her aching heart.

When they arrived in Pittsburgh, they carried their bags through the motel lobby. The routine unfolded. Ride up the elevator, wait for the ding, put one foot in front of the other, put the key into the door, quiet the kids, and pray they would not disturb the other rooms.

Again, and again, like the Israelites wandering the desert, they longed for entrance to the Promised land.

There was no sign in Pennsylvania, other than a moment when Terri said Kathryn Kuhlman came to her in a vision and imparted her anointing to her. Tamara witnessed no evidence of such anointing, but hoped that something had transpired by going to Pittsburgh.

They stayed one night, and then they were off to New Castle.

At the next motel, Uncle Anthony entertained the kids with a puppet show behind a folded-up cot, using Annie's baby doll and a sock for a puppet.

It felt good to hear the kids laugh for a change.

They had many nights of fighting and bickering. The children continued to ask questions the three adults had no answers to. "God is going to take care of us" was all they could say.

Blind faith for these little ones! They were at the mercy of the adults who were leading them. If their leaders were indeed deceived, what would become of them?

They were all at the mercy of God Himself. What was the true way to take their children safely through this life and eventually into eternity?

A man named Thomas in the Bible had questioned Jesus about the same thing,

"Lord, we do not know where you are going; how can we know the way?" John 14:5 (NIV)

Jesus responded to Tamara the same way He responded to Thomas: "I am the way, and the truth, and the life; no one comes to the Father, but by me." John 14:6 (NIV)

The way became clear only as she followed Jesus in obedience, moment-by-moment, and breath-by-breath.

CHAPTER 22

Then you will know the truth, and the truth will set you free.
~John 8:32 NIV

ALTHOUGH TRAVELING FARTHER AWAY IN BODY EACH DAY, TAMARA'S mind and soul remained in the grip of the past, replaying every ugly scene.

The nights in the motels were incredibly long.

~

PAST (SAM CALLS A MEETING 1988)

"YOUR FATHER WANTS A MEETING." VICTORIA SAID CALMLY OVER the phone to Tamara.

Victoria had moved back in with Sam after leaving him for a short period of time, announcing to her children that she was not going to give up all they had worked for. And, the zinger, which no one dared challenge; God had asked her to return to him and love him into the kingdom of God. Their mountain home was prophesied to be where they would all survive the end of the world. To fulfill prophesy, she must live on the mountain.

Tamara understood that her mother wanted to bring Sam into the Kingdom of God, but she was confused. Why would her mother move back in, when he made no steps towards repentance, and even denied what he had done?

Shouldn't she pray for him from afar until she witnessed a change? A little remorse?

Why couldn't she see that Sam was not concerned about the condition of his daughter? His family? The only emotion displayed was about his own preservation!

Tamara's grip on the phone tightened as she called her sister Terri.

"Oh, hi Tamara, what's up?"

"It's about Dad. He wants us to all meet. He has something he wants to tell us. Maybe he is ready to admit what he has done and wants to ask your forgiveness!" exclaimed Tamara.

The other end of the line grew silent.

"Terri, you there?" asked Tamara.

"Yeah, I'm here." Terri choked. "Do you think that's what he really wants to get together about?"

"We can only hope." responded Tamara. "Meet me here at my house around Four o'clock and we'll ride down together."

TAMARA FELT AN INTENSE UNEASINESS AS SHE WALKED INTO THE family room, but she silently prayed to hold it back.

Her father leaned back on the bright red sectional with Victoria poised to his right. Terri entered behind Tamara, and Sam sat forward, folding his hands.

The familiar twitch in his tightened jaw, and the glare in his eyes told Tamara immediately that this was not an invitation to a reconciliation.

Sam cleared his throat and spoke in a low angry tone, sending chills down Tamara's spine.

"I've been talking to the good Lord about this lie in our family. I am going to go on a 3 day fast. God is going to show who the liar is!"

"Dad, you know you raped me! Why can't you just admit it?" Terri burst into tears.

"Get out of my house!" Sam bellowed.

Tamara hurried to Terri's side, whispering, "Now God can work. Don't you see, Dad has given God permission to show who the liar is!"

As they left their parent's home, Terri reminded Tamara of the word that God had given her seven months prior. It was from an obscure verse in the Bible that mentioned the seventh month. She had told Tamara that she believed God would reveal the truth within the seventh month from when she blew the whistle on the incest in their childhood home.

Nodding, Tamara said, "Oh my gosh! I *do* remember you telling me that, and three days from now is the end of the seventh month!"

This was not mere coincidence. They had never mentioned it to anyone else. Sam could not have known this prophetic word, or was it a prophetic curse?

THE SECOND DAY OF SAM'S FASTING, VICTORIA CALLED TAMARA. "You girls better get over here, your father's deathly ill. I have to get him to the hospital!"

They rushed to their parent's home to find an ambulance parked in front. The paramedics had their father on a stretcher.

Sam lay there, skin ashen and sweaty, breathing shallow. They had seen their father, a diabetic, in the state of insulin shock before, but it was unsettling nonetheless.

Tamara and Terri ran to their mother crying. They both loved him, despite his wickedness. They didn't want him to die, but to live, so their family could be restored. That had been their prayer all along, not to condemn him, but to forgive him. Tamara believed it was God's perfect will and it would be done!

Victoria fell apart while they followed the ambulance to the hospital. "I need him!" she cried.

Tamara was stunned that within a few months, Victoria had gone from hating him, and calling him trash, to desperately needing him.

CHAPTER 23

You will be betrayed even by parents, brothers and sisters, relatives
and friends, and they will put some of you to death. Everyone will
hate you because of me. But not a hair of your head will perish.
Stand firm, and you will win life. ~Luke 21:16-19 NIV

PAST 1988

TAMARA AND TERRI SAT SILENTLY IN THE WAITING ROOM AT THE
hospital. Their older sister Becky approached with a look of disdain.
"This has been too much on Dad, I don't believe any of this is
true!"

Tamara's mind reeled. They had been dubbed the
troublemakers of the family. To deal with the truth of what they
were raised in, Becky had chosen the easier route of denial,
becoming a hollow, religious robot.

No pain to walk through, and no joy. Her eyes betrayed the
emptiness in her soul.

Sometimes Tamara wanted to take her older sister's pulse to see if she was even alive.

Terri's story had made it full circle by now, and as relatives and friends entered the room, their looks and whispers became intolerable.

How were *they* the bad guys in all of this?

"Pay no attention to them Terri," Tamara whispered in her sister's ear.

They got up from their chairs and sought the hospital chapel for refuge. As they opened the door of the chapel, they saw their mother Victoria sprawled across the carpeted floor, her breathing erratic.

"Mom!" they cried. "What are you doing? Are you okay?"

They dropped to their knees, and leaned over their mother.

"I'm praying. God told me to breathe for Sam," gasped Victoria. She immediately went back into the deep erratic breaths.

Terri and Tamara held hands and prayed. It was all too spooky and weird! They cried out for the life of their father, and the sanity of their mother.

LATER THAT EVENING, SAM'S DOCTOR APPROACHED VICTORIA. "Do you have a Pastor or Priest you'd like to call? Your husband's body is breaking down into the death stages. I don't think he will live through the night."

Terri crumbled, "Oh God, I just want him to say he is sorry, I don't want him to die!"

Tamara joined Terri in begging God to spare his life.

By the end of the third day Sam was in a coma and hooked to life support. For the next two weeks he remained in a diabetic coma. Anthony flew in from California to be with them.

The next days were a flurry of prayer and conversation at the hospital. Tamara's heart broke as she heard Terri whisper, "God, I should be the one in that bed."

Tamara realized that Terri wished herself dead, rather than to feel she was the cause of Sam's death.

They prayed that the coma be a place for Sam to encounter the true Messiah, that when he awoke, they could be a family again.

ONE MORNING VICTORIA CALLED TAMARA, "YOUR FATHERS AWAKE. I need to go home for a shower and change of clothes but should be back in a couple of hours, you kids wait for me."

Tamara couldn't get to the hospital fast enough! Rushing into the front entrance, she met Anthony and Terri. "Do you think he is different?" Terri asked.

"We sure hope so, something had to have happened during all that time!" said Anthony.

"Mom wanted us to wait for her, but I just couldn't." said Terri.

"I know, I couldn't wait either." said Tamara.

The three decided to have Terri go in first, alone.

After waiting awhile, they finally joined Terri by their father's bedside. Tamara was startled at the sight of Sam. He looked worse than ever. His face was hollow, gray skin stretched across a skeleton. Darkness encircled his sunken, lifeless eyes. He made a feeble attempt to smile as they neared him.

She leaned forward to kiss his cheek and with one glance towards Terri's chair, she saw that their talk had not gone well. Terri sat somberly with her head down.

"Ter..." before Tamara could get her name out, Terri ran from the room.

Tamara followed her to the bathroom. Terri was sobbing on the other side of the stall door. "I went to him and told him that I loved him and was so glad he came through, and he just looked at me and said, 'I've got my family back now, but we've still got this lie.'"

Tamara shuddered at his words. *How can he still say that?* she thought.

They had all been faithfully praying for Sam, praying that he would encounter God during the coma, and he'd come to the truth about everything. They prayed that he would see that he had been following a false messiah.

How could he not see that he was given a second chance at life to make things right?

TAMARA INVITED ANTHONY AND TERRI OVER FOR COFFEE. THEY SAT under a blanket of despair. They had contended for so long. Their world shattered all over again.

Their relatives and friends were convinced that they lied about a good and godly man, and it was *their* fault his health had failed.

The Pastor they had gone to for help in their new Spirit filled church even stood by their father, whom he had only known for a short time.

No one would deal with the situation in the churches they attended. It seemed Sam had committed the perfect murder; killing his children's innocence and hiding the evidence in the church where it could never be unearthed, and there was no digging allowed!

Sam knew the Bible from Genesis to Revelation. He knew how to hide within its pages, twisting the Scriptures to his own destruction. He had many well-meaning Christians back him up, fully confident they served God by admonishing Sam's family, and comforting him.

LATER THAT EVENING TAMARA LAY ON THE LIVING ROOM FLOOR with her Bible open. She poured out her confusion, *God, why is there no help from Your church?* The Lord led her to the fourth chapter of Ecclesiastes.

King Solomon spoke what Tamara felt.

"Again, I observed all the oppression under the sun. I saw the tears of the oppressed, with no one to comfort them. The oppressor's have great power, their victims are helpless." Eccl. 4:1 (NIV)

Tamara wept. In this insane world, she found solace and understanding in God's Word alone.

~

Instead of coming back from the brink of death a changed man, Sam's presence was more steeped in evil than ever.

Tamara wondered if cheating death made him feel more invincible?

She felt the same demonic pull towards him that she had felt since childhood, after he would abuse her. Recovering their relationship after his verbal and physical blows was always on her. After being beaten she was to make amends.

Sam's repentance was never a requirement for her to come close to him, he simply demanded her trust and loyalty. His disapproval was unbearable, and the devil drew her back into her father's lair through her longing to be loved by him. Tamara had been a willing, but ignorant party in perpetuating the abusive cycles in the family.

Until now.

Although she felt the familiar wicked pull to her Father, the Lord Jesus enabled her to resist it. Greater was Jesus in her, than Satan and his demons in the world.

CHAPTER 24

But you will not leave in haste or go in flight; for the LORD will go
before you, the God of Israel will be your rear guard.
~Isaiah 52:12 NIV

PRESENT 1989

AFTER A MONTH OF RUNNING, THE THREE ADULTS CAME TO THE
stark realization that they could not go on like this. They prayed
long into the night, and the decision was unanimous.

They had to return to their hometown.

After breakfast, Terri sat cross legged on the bed and picked up
the phone, laying the cradle in her lap. Anthony and Tamara
gathered around her atop the brown floral bedspread.

They sent Tamara's oldest son Brandon down to the lobby with
the other kids to get some treats, so they would have some private
uninterrupted time.

Tamara and her siblings had prayed all along for restoration of their families. Perhaps God had moved in their absence. Whatever the case, they must go back and get custody of their children if nothing had changed. They would have to confront the mountain in their lives.

"Hello." Terri seemed unaffected by her husband's voice on the other end of the line.

She coldly recounted to him all he had done to her children.

Anthony and Tamara could not believe their ears as Terri held the phone out for them to listen to Ray's plea, "Please God no, I want my family back! I'll do anything! Please forgive me!"

Would it be that easy? Had the time of not knowing where his family was brought about a change of heart?

Terri knew how cunning and deceitful Ray could be so she proceeded with her inquiry. "Alicia described a time when I went to the store and you were in the shower when I left. She said that you came out in a towel. If you want to ever see us again, you need to finish telling me what happened, just like Alicia said."

Ray recounted everything identical to Alicia's story while he sobbed into the phone. In between each detail Ray cried out, "Forgive me Jesus! I don't want to go to prison!"

Terri promised that if he would confess and go to counseling, they could be a family again. She would not press any charges.

She hung up and handed the phone to Tamara, "Your turn."

Tamara's fear of Brent almost equaled the fear of her father. Trembling, she dialed her own number. ".........Brent, it's me."

"Oh honey," he gushed, "I have been worried sick about you. You need to come home! This craziness with your family has got to end!"

Tamara continued, "Brent, the boys shared some things."

"What?" he said incredulously, "Oh honey, you're so mixed up! All these accusations, you are just confused. I don't think your dad did anything to Terri either."

Tamara stopped for a moment as doubts swirled. A spirit of confusion hovered over her mind. She felt the familiar shaking that always led her away from the confidence of what she knew.

Praying under her breath, she told him that she was coming

back, but they could not be a family again unless he confessed to abusing the boys and got counseling.

"Honey, I love my family and I'll *do* anything, even counseling, to have you and my boys back. Just come home!"

Tamara covered the phone as the children burst into the room.

"Who are you talking to Mommy?" asked her son Joshua.

"Your dad." Tamara replied.

The evening prior, they had explained to the children that they needed to return to their hometown and go through the courts to get custody. They hoped that being away had changed their father's hearts, and if not, they were going to file for divorce. Either way, they assured them that God had exposed darkness and they would be safe. Their moms would protect them.

The boys crowded around the phone, "What is he saying? Is he mad at us?"

Inquiring young eyes searched their mother's face.

"No, he is not mad. He says that he loves us and will go through family counseling to have us back together."

Aaron stepped towards the phone, "I want to talk to Dad."

Hesitantly, she handed the phone over. Tamara could hear Brent's emotional interaction with their son, telling him how much he loved and missed them all, and how sorry he was for what they had been through. He assured him he was not mad and they just needed to come home.

"Daddy's sorry Mommy. He's different now. We can go home!" Aaron said with a smile.

The children missed their home and friends, and still loved their Dad.

Tamara felt sick as she ended the call. Her stomach clenched at the realization she had to see him when they returned. She too, still felt some love for him, but how could she love a monster?

CHAPTER 25

Do not suppose that I have come to bring peace to the earth. I did
not come to bring peace, but a sword. For I have come to turn a
man against his father, a daughter against her mother, a daughter-
in-law against her mother-in-law- a man's enemies will be the
members of his own household. ~Matthew 10:34-36 NIV

ANTHONY LOADED UP HIS SISTER'S AND THEIR CHILDREN INTO THE
little compact car they had rented and began the long trek from
Pennsylvania to their hometown. It was early morning as they made
their way through a blizzard that hit in the middle of the night.
Anthony could barely make out the road in front of them. As they
inched their way along the highway, Tamara prayed. White snowfall
clouded their view. Although it was not the darkness that had clung
to the windows on the way down the mountain a month earlier, it
was still unclear as to what lay ahead.

It seemed their path would remain obscure. They were going
back, but to what? The houses they left were no more. They could
not remain the same. One of three things would happen.

Repentance and healing, divorce, or denial and even deeper deception.

Tamara lay her head back on the seat, her leg cramping where a child sprawled across her. Eight of them in a car built for five at maximum capacity.

Discomfort, physically and emotionally.

No way to escape it. The only way was through it.

Long hours on the road loomed ahead of them, with tired and worn out children who had no idea what the past month had really been all about. What about their new start? What about Disneyland?

CHAPTER 26

What are you doing, you devastated one? Why dress yourself in
scarlet and put on jewels of gold? Why highlight your eyes with
makeup? You adorn yourself in vain. Your lovers despise you; they
want to kill you. ~Jeremiah 4:30 NIV

ARRIVING BACK AT TERRI'S APARTMENT, RAY CAME RUNNING OUT,
sweeping his wife and children into his arms. It made Tamara's skin
crawl. She wanted to see a happy reunion, an answer to prayers for
Ray to change, but she saw only a facade.

The familiar uneasiness crept upon her, a sick feeling that things
weren't ever going to be right. But oh, how she hoped she was
wrong!

Anthony unloaded their bags and said his goodbyes. He needed
to return the rental car and schedule a flight back to repair his job
and life in California.

As Tamara applied her make-up while getting ready to see
Brent, she was so apprehensive she could barely breathe. She hated
herself for making sure she looked her best before seeing him. The

monster had been revealed, so why would she still care if she was attractive to him?

The boys played outside while waiting for their father. Familiar ground was a relief to them.

When Brent got off work, he came to pick them up. Tamara dreaded going back to their home on the mountain, but her religious thoughts kicked in. *He wants to reconcile, to save our marriage and get counseling. He acts like he's sorry. All of those testimonies of horrible people changing into godly men and women. God hates divorce...*

The spiritual realm of darkness was already at work through a religious spirit to take her and her boys' captive again.

Brent's enthusiasm equaled Ray's upon seeing his family. "Oh, how I've missed you. You look so good!" Brent swung Tamara into his arms.

His hug was as dead and empty as her father's had been that day on her porch the year before. Her heart sank, she knew immediately this was wrong.

As they neared their mountain home, the boys sat quietly in the back seat.

Tamara felt ill. *What was she doing?* She tangibly felt the atmosphere change as oppression rolled over her.

God help me! Protect us Lord Jesus! she prayed silently as they wound up their road.

Walking in her front door was like walking into the jaws of Hell itself. Brent's grinning face said it all.

He thinks he's won.

After settling the kids into bed, Brent and Tamara sat down to talk.

Brent leaned into her, stroking her face and hair, "I love you so much, you know that don't you?"

Tamara felt faint, "I know Brent, but..." she was terrified to utter the next words, "Are you going to get counseling like you promised?"

Brent stiffened, and sat back, she could see the anger rise. His kind act had always been a paper-thin mask.

How had she believed it was love for so many years? One

moment he took steel toed boots to her head, smeared her dinner plate into her hair, and cursed her very existence. In the next moment, he swept her into his arms, and kissed her bloodied face, vowing to never harm her again.

She had seen it all and lived it all before.

A country singer's voice had streamed loudly from her parents record player, telling a woman to stand by her man. It had been a theme in her home as a child, and even as Christians, this theme played.

"Tamara." Brent said through pursed lips, "You and your sister and brother went a little nutty, Ray and I had to agree to anything to get you back here!"

"Brent, I know the kids didn't make that stuff up. If you just admit it and get help, God can heal you."

Why couldn't she just say it straight forward! Why was she playing nice? Petrifying fear stopped her from a full-blown confrontation. She knew she had to get her boys safely away from him, this time for good.

Brent looked at her with a sickening smile, "Honey, I forgive you for taking my boys and leaving. We can forget all of this, I don't care what people think, I have my family back and that's all that matters."

"I'm really tired Brent, I have to get some sleep" she said.

God get us through this night, I know I shouldn't have come back, forgive me. I wanted to believe he'd change Lord. You know my heart. Please, deliver us!

She had to continue the facade for the evening and not threaten to leave. He already vowed he would see her dead if she ever left him, and now he had her back. She didn't dare defy him openly.

She thought back to one time in particular when she threatened to leave him, only to wake up with him gently caressing her head, and stroking her hair. She looked up at him, perplexed, and he had simply smiled, "Do you know how close I came to grabbing my gun and blowing your head off last night?"

The terror that gripped her then gripped her now.

∾

"Please, I just need some time," she pleaded with Brent as she pushed his hands away.

He jumped up from the bed, turning towards the bathroom, and suddenly whirled around with his fist in the air, "If I ever touched one of my boys wrong or did anything to them, may God strike me dead!"

Tamara braced herself, truly believing that at any moment lightning would strike.

How could he be so arrogant? she thought.

Brent slept on the couch, something he had only done one time before. Tamara knew it was God's grace to her.

As she lay in bed, her mind raced. How had she gotten herself back into this? She knew she had to leave again, but it couldn't be like before. She had to pray and think it out. She would leave in the morning, when Brent left for work on the day shift at the factory.

When Brent stayed home the next day, it left Tamara in sheer panic. She needed to leave! The minutes ticked by, one of the longest days of Tamara's life.

"I'll go and get a pizza for us." said Brent that evening.

"That sounds great." Tamara tried not to sound too anxious. Her heart quickened, thankful he was leaving. She could grab the kids and be gone before he got back.

"Aaron, get your coat, you're going with dad to get pizza." he yelled down the hallway.

God. No! thought Tamara, but she knew she would only tip Brent off if she said Aaron couldn't go.

As they pulled out of the driveway, Tamara prayed fervently. Brent had challenged God and she feared for his life. She didn't want her son's anywhere near him without her!

When the phone rang twenty minutes after they left, adrenaline shot through her body.

"Hello, Mrs. Sawyer, this is the Police Department. Do you have a moment?"

Tears sprang from Tamara's eyes and tortured thoughts tumbled through her mind before the officer could get another word out.

Was there a car wreck? God, did you strike Brent? What about Aaron?

"Ma'am, we wondered if you would like to purchase two tickets to the circus to support the families of our fallen officers."

"Ah, yeah, sure." Tamara gave him her information.

Tamara broke down sobbing after she hung up. She had lived on the raw edge for so long, she felt she couldn't take much more before she cracked.

She heard God would not give her more than she could handle, but how many times had her heart and mind challenged the truth of that?

She managed to muster up enough courage to act normal when they returned with the pizza, making a few comments about the upcoming week. She desperately needed him to go to work and knew he had to feel secure that she was back.

It worked.

Brent went back to work the next day. If she had ever felt she lost the trust of her children, it was now. As she loaded her kids into the car, she was met with angry words.

"Why are we leaving again Mom?" Joshua asked. "Dad said we are going to go play ball at the park this weekend!"

Aaron chimed in, "Dad is different now! He is sorry for being mean to us. Now you're being mean!"

Brandon threw a few choice words at Tamara, cursing her for bringing them back to that house.

"I know that we shouldn't have come back. Please forgive me. Your father said he'd get help, but he was lying."

She struggled incredibly under the weight of her decisions as she headed back toward her sister's apartment. What did the future hold?

CHAPTER 27

H<small>E</small> <small>REPLIED</small> <small>TO</small> <small>HIM</small>, "W<small>HO</small> <small>IS</small> <small>MY</small> <small>MOTHER</small>, <small>AND</small> <small>WHO</small> <small>ARE</small> <small>MY</small> brothers?" Pointing to his disciples, he said, "Here are my mother and my brothers. For whoever does the will of my Father in heaven is my brother and sister and mother. ~Matthew 12:48-50 NIV

W<small>HEN</small> <small>SHE</small> <small>ARRIVED</small> <small>BACK</small> <small>AT</small> <small>HER</small> <small>SISTER'S</small> <small>APARTMENT</small>, T<small>AMARA</small> <small>GOT</small> her boys settled into the tiny room they had to share with their cousins. Finally, she sat down with her sister in the kitchen, coffee cup in hand.

"I knew Brent wouldn't truly come around Tamara."

"Well, do you believe Ray is sincere?" Tamara asked.

"Yes, I'm taking the children into a counselor tomorrow and he is going with us."

"That is so wonderful Terri. I'm so happy for you!"

While adding creamer to her coffee, Tamara continued, "I have to hire a lawyer soon, I have no other option than divorce, and I'm taking the boys to talk to the police tomorrow."

That afternoon while Terri watched the kids, Tamara visited a dear friend's house.

Tamara had led her friend Kathy to the Lord and loved her dearly, but things had gotten so crazy, and they had left so suddenly that she hadn't been able to say goodbye. Even if she had said goodbye, what would she have said? They had no answers at the time, they only knew things had to *drastically* change.

As Tamara drove up Kathy's familiar driveway, her heart swelled. She had missed her friend. Kathy was such a young Christian. Tamara knew she would not have the capacity to understand all that had taken place and that another realm was at work. As she walked up the steps, she saw her friends face appear behind the screen door, "Kathy!" Tamara exclaimed, eager to hug her friend.

Kathy stepped forward and with great sadness quietly said, "Tamara, it's so nice to see you, but...."

Tamara stopped in her tracks, nausea engulfing her. Brent and the church had gotten to Kathy.

"I can't let you in my house." Kathy's words confirmed her suspicions.

Tamara could no longer fight the tears, "Why not?"

"Brent called, he told us you left again. You need to go back to him."

"But Kathy," Tamara's words trembled with emotion, "He molested two of my boys and he's not sorry. He is still denying everything."

Kathy broke in, "It doesn't matter what you think he's done. You need to save your marriage. Forgive him and go back."

Tamara had taught Kathy well, and led Bible studies in her home. She taught that God hates divorce and no sin is unforgivable except blaspheming the Holy Spirit. Now it was being quoted to her.

Did she forget to mention that there needed to be *repentance* with action on the part of the perpetrator?

The church Terri and Tamara attended before leaving was the one Kathy was now very much involved in. Tamara herself had invited her there! The Pastor counseled the congregation to shun Tamara until she returned to her husband.

Tamara stood bewildered at the door.

Kathy's husband pulled into the driveway and made his way to Kathy's side, attempting to close the door in Tamara's face, "You need to leave now Tamara."

Tamara numbly walked to her car and drove away, devastation settling on her.

She no longer had a voice for Christ in her own hometown.

CHAPTER 28

So, do not be afraid of them, for there is nothing concealed that will
not be disclosed, or hidden that will not be made known.
~Matthew 10:26 NIV

At the police department, Tamara's boys spoke with a
counselor one at a time. After what seemed an eternity, the
counselor asked Tamara to join her in her office.

"Your son Aaron said his father has never done anything to him,
except that he was mean."

Tamara felt her face flush. Why had Aaron not told her the
truth?

"And as for your son Joshua, he told me that he lay down with
dad during naptime and Daddy rubbed up against him. Then he
said that he saw a demon in the room." The counselor sat back,
staring at Tamara as if she were a freak. "What is it that you teach
your children anyway?"

Tamara knew she could not speak of spiritual things to someone who would not understand. Joshua had indeed seen a demon, but she could not convince this woman of that.

The counselor went on, "I'm sorry, we don't have enough evidence to proceed with any criminal charges against your husband."

Despair enveloped Tamara. Why had they come back?

She thought she was coming back for restoration and that justice would prevail!

When they got back home the television was broadcasting a news bulletin about a woman who fled with her daughter from an abusive husband, to another country.

The volume seemed to increase without her turning it up, "The courts granted custody to the father, finding no evidence of sexual abuse. The mother now faces prosecution if she does not return to the United States."

A still small voice came to Tamara.

Justice is not from man.

She knew what God was conveying to her. She and her boys would not find justice on the earth, but they would find it in God.

CHAPTER 29

You suffered along with those in prison and joyfully accepted the confiscation of your property, because you knew that you yourselves had better and lasting possessions. ~Hebrews 10:34 NIV

A FEW WEEKS LATER, TAMARA STARTED THE PROCESS FOR DIVORCE.

She went into her sister Terri's bedroom and called Brent. They needed to discuss the division of property. Brent soon shifted the conversation and pleaded with Tamara to get rid of her lawyer, and return to their home. Tamara became momentarily disoriented, realizing how crazy their trip had looked to *everyone*.

She was tempted to agree with Brent. After all, they were homeless, she had no job and no skills to start over. Maybe they had gone a bit nuts and maybe it was *all* a lie.

Suddenly, her thoughts were interrupted by a strong rebuke deep in her Spirit,

The blood of your children is on your head if you go back!

The fear of God in that moment gave her strength to never again lean into an easier way, the way of deception.

"Brent, I am going through with the divorce. If you have anything further to say to me, do it through our lawyers."

"Fine with me, but you will get nothing else from this house. If you don't come back, I am getting rid of your stuff, you won't get any of it!"

"I just want the chest with the pictures of the kids. Please Brent!"

"You will never get a single picture Tamara." And with that, he hung up the phone.

A POEM SPILLED FORTH, IN RED INK FROM HER BLEEDING HEART:

When darkness overtook her, and she wanted to leave this place,
God showed her a picture and she studied each little face,
"It's for their lives you're fighting" came God's still small voice,
"You're blazing a trail for your children, that they will have a choice,
that generational sins not be their lot,
though ancient snares set long ago, they will not be caught!"
Now rising from self-pity, she stood upon God's Word,
And began putting into practice all that she'd read and heard!

BRENT FOLLOWED THROUGH ON HIS WORD. HER PERSONAL ITEMS and the home she'd built over the years were gone, sold at garage sales.

But her soul was no longer up for sale.

CHAPTER 30

So, justice is driven back, and righteousness stands at a distance; truth has stumbled in the streets, honesty cannot enter.
~ Isaiah 59:14 NIV

Court was in the morning.

Tamara tried to sleep, but it alluded her. She lay on her sister's living room floor, in anguish over the words she had just read; a pile of affidavits sent from her divorce lawyer sat beside her.

People she loved and invested in most of her life, and others from her church congregation had written letters for Brent to get custody of her boys.

They all too readily penned how they had seen Tamara go too deep into spirituality, and how the children would be better off with Brent.

The sickening feelings of betrayal overwhelmed her as she read lies with smatterings of truth. The words now played repeatedly in her pounding head.

She knew how crazy it had all appeared with her leaving town.

But why didn't anyone stick up for her? Didn't they know her better than that?

Why did they not remember the times she had rushed to their aid, taught Bible studies, or cried and prayed by their sides?

Her history of life with Brent was well known to them all: his drunken and drugged rages, womanizing and abusive ways. They were long a subject of rumor in their town. She had even been advised repeatedly by Brent's own family to leave him.

The misery that surged through her body was almost unbearable. Since rededicating her life to Christ, living for Jesus and loving people had become her lifelong pursuit. All of her influence seemed to have slipped away in one month.

Without her there to explain herself, she had been judged, found guilty and deemed unfit to raise her own children.

She cried while sitting among the condemning papers until she was spent. But what came next was a sorrow she had never known.

Her mind exploded with the thought that if Brent got custody of her sons, it was all in vain! The run for their lives was only a mockery. The very idea of her sons being taken from her and put into her husband's hands was too much.

A silent screaming pain erupted from her soul. Her body convulsed as she cried out to God, "I need Your help! Can't You hear me?!"

Immediately she heard God speak into her Spirit, *Psalm 3:4*

She dragged herself over to her Bible and the words sprang forth, like an oasis in the desert.

"To the Lord I cry aloud, and he answers me from his holy mountain. I lie down and sleep because the Lord sustains me, I will not fear the tens of thousands drawn up against me on every side." (Psalm 3:4)

Blessed relief swept over Tamara. She knew that God had heard her and He was on her side, no matter who was against her!

She went to sleep in peace and awakened the next morning feeling an invisible shield around her. Although there was a fear that she continually held off through prayer, she felt the encompassing presence and peace of her God.

At the courthouse the next morning, she reminded herself of a higher court in session. As she exited the elevator and stepped onto her floor, she glanced up towards the courtroom doors.

The sight made her catch her breath.

She continued on.

Only her silent prayer language calmed her.

Brent's family was lined up on the bench just outside the courtroom, their stares already pronouncing a harsh sentence on her.

As she walked past them, she drew in a deep breath, and inwardly recited, *I will not fear tens of thousands drawn up against me.*

"Your honor," Brent's high paid lawyer began the proceedings. "My client Brent Sawyer has spent the last month worried sick about his wife and children. His wife has gone over the edge spiritually, as you can read in the affidavits I sent you. One is even from her last Pastor. Mrs. Sawyer even claims to have visions from God," he said, dramatically sweeping his hands into the air.

"She has poisoned her children with lies about their father and we seek full custody for the well-being of their two sons, Joshua and Aaron. Brent is *not* seeking custody of Brandon, as he is not the biological father."

Tamara trusted God to give her favor with the judge, but her heart sank as she realized her oldest son was being thrown out like the trash. Brent had raised Brandon from the time he could say Daddy, but now he meant nothing to him.

Obviously, Tamara did not want him to get custody, but knew Brandon would find out that Brent did not even care enough to fight for him.

Her mind reflected upon the warped portrayals of her in the pile of affidavits. She wouldn't even give herself custody if she didn't know the truth! She thought especially of the Pastor's letter, full of outright lies without an inkling of truth. She sighed and leaned into her Savior.

Tamara's attorney was up next. He started by mocking the

Pastor's letter and told how his church was actually under investigation as a cult.

More puzzle pieces clicked into place in Tamara's mind. More deception was unraveling, more truth of what she had unwittingly been submitting to in the name of the Lord.

Her lawyer went on to explain that the reason Tamara left was due to fear for her and her children's safety. He explained Brent's rage and abuse, asking for full custody with no contact with their father.

After hearing both sides, the Judge leaned forward and put his hand squarely on the stack of affidavits, "I am not going to waste my time reading these. Anybody could have written anything. I see nothing unfit about this woman. However, I also do not have enough evidence to prevent Brent from seeing his children. I am granting custody to the mother with unrestricted visitation for the father."

Tamara's relief was mixed. She had seen God move this judge's heart in her favor. She had custody of her sons, but Brent still had access to them!

God gently reminded her again, *Deliverance is not from man*!

CHAPTER 31

Those who look to him are radiant; their faces are never covered
with shame.
~Psalm 34:5 NIV

As Tamara waited in the welfare office, she felt a familiar
wave of sickness as she scanned the room. Memories filled with
shame flooded her soul. Years earlier she had sat in this very office,
an unwed teen mother. She felt she had deserved it then, leading a
life of drinking and promiscuity. But now? She had always longed
for the honor of being a married woman and believed that her
marriage to Brent would be redeemed. That they would live happily
ever after.

Now here she was, a Christian woman, back where she had
started, asking for money and food to feed her children.

She had no idea how to feel honored as a woman without a ring
on her finger, especially with kids.

Memories of the condescending stares of people at her Baptist
church, as an unwed teen mom, still bore into her soul. The one

time someone from her congregation reached out was only be a ploy for her to give them her child.

Please God, Tamara prayed, *let me have a nice Social Worker. I can't take any more.*

"Tamara Sawyer!" Hearing her name propelled her forward.

She rose from the chair, her legs shaking and followed the elderly social worker to a back room.

"Do you have all of your paperwork in order?"

"I think so. Is this all I need?" Tamara asked, handing her the papers.

"And where are your children's birth certificates?" the caseworker snapped.

"Uh, I don't have all of that right now. I'm not able to access those because I can't go to my home. My husband is violent."

"Well," the worker said, "I don't think there is a thing we can do for you until you get us those documents. You people just think you can waltz in here unprepared."

The words pelted Tamara like stones.

I just wanted someone to be nice to me, she cried silently to God.

Tamara could not hold back the flood of tears that came next.

The caseworker rose from her chair, grabbed a tissue box and rushed to her side. "Oh honey. Here, take this, I'll see what I can do. I didn't mean to make you cry!"

The compassion that poured from the woman in the next half hour let Tamara know that God indeed had given her a nice person, just as she had asked.

Tamara walked out of that office with an emergency check on its way and food stamps to feed her children. She thanked the Lord, not only for the provision, but for his forgiveness of her judgment of Him.

God's comfort washed over her as she sat behind the wheel, rays of sun, breaking through the clouds and bathing her face. She felt His radiance replacing shame as her covering.

CHAPTER 32

BUT BECAUSE MY SERVANT CALEB HAS A DIFFERENT SPIRIT AND follows me wholeheartedly, I will bring him into the land he went to, and his descendants will inherit it. ~Numbers 14:24 NIV

TAMARA AND HER BOYS MOVED OUT OF HER SISTER'S APARTMENT AND into town after she'd saved enough for her first month's rent. She'd gone to the store without a thought for so many years, but now it became an unnerving event. Her friends stood aloof and people whispered and stared.

Although she could not hear she was sure of their words, "There's Tamara, she went crazy. I read about what she put her poor husband through in the newspaper!"

Every time, she rushed home to her Bible and found the perfect words to sooth her tattered soul.

"My life is consumed by anguish and my years by groaning.... because of all my enemies I am the utter contempt of my neighbors, I am a dread to my friends, those who see me on the street flee from me." Psalm 31:10

The streetlights outside of her apartment flooded into her room each night, so utterly different than the deep darkness of their mountain home. Nights were still something she feared, so even artificial light brought relief.

But still, the occasional weird events invaded her apartment. Most evenings, for the first few months, as Tamara drifted off to sleep, she heard her son's panicked voice, "Mom, flip the tape over!"

Her son Aaron could not sleep without worship music playing softly in his room. Once the tape reached its end, so did her son's peace. He was targeted in particular with night terrors and demonic visitations.

She stayed in her hometown for three months, until she and her sister attended a Pentecostal Spirit filled church just across the river. Terri's husband Ray was offered a job in the same town soon after, so a move was imminent.

The new Pastor's sermons spoke life into Tamara, and she instantly fell in love with the community.

Soon after joining the church, Tamara was invited to a singles retreat. Her divorce was not finalized but she longed for fellowship.

The retreat was full of laughter and relaxation. Things had been so hard for so long it was just what she needed. Although she relished the attention of Christian men, she clung to an older woman she met there named Sandy, who quickly took Tamara under her wing.

The first day, a tall handsome man greeted her. "Hi, my name is Tom. What church are you from?"

"Hi, I'm Tamara. I just recently starting attending Mountainview." she answered warily.

"Wow, really? I attend there but I have never seen you!" he grinned.

"Not surprising in a church of five thousand!" she smiled back.

Tom followed the ladies to lunch, snapping up a seat to the left of her new friend Sandy, who began her motherly lecture. "Tamara is not on the market Tom! She is going through a divorce."

Tom chuckled and hugged Tamara's bodyguard. "Relax Mom, I am not hitting on her!"

Over lunch, Tom shared the things God laid on his heart

through Scripture, and Tamara was awed by his insight. As the afternoon wore on, they took a stroll by the river, and Tamara became more impressed.

Tom was the perfect Christian gentleman. The three became inseparable. Sandy, also quite taken with Tom, adopted him like a son.

At the end of the retreat, they exchanged phone numbers and made plans to attend church together. It felt good to establish some new friendships.

Things were looking up!

TERRI AND RAY MOVED ACROSS THE RIVER TO PLEASURE, OREGON and Terri invited Tamara to come live with them. Tamara was hesitant at first, but loved the thought of being in the same town as her new church. After much prayer, God gave Tamara a scripture.

"Before them fire devours, behind them a flame blazes. Before them the land is like the garden of Eden, behind them, a desert waste, nothing escapes them." Joel 2:3

With that, she packed up their meager belongings and moved in with her sister.

Tamara's last load was packed to the brim in her little car, and she sang along with the Praise music on her cassette tape, so full of joy. Her new friend Tom sat beside her, helping her with the move. She was heading towards more freedom!

Just as she left the city limits, she heard a loud *pop* and her car rolled to a stop, dead. Tom jumped out to steer the car to the side of the road. He opened the hood and said, "How Weird! Your battery has a crack in it!"

She had just replaced the battery a month earlier.

They walked back to an auto repair shop that was only a quarter mile away. The owner graciously towed her vehicle back to his shop to look at it. He too was perplexed at what he saw, confirming how rare it was for a new battery to simply burst.

Within a couple hours, they were back on the road and Tamara was one step closer to her new life. As she drove past the city limits, she sensed the battery bursting was a territorial principality's last attempt to thwart her moving away from her place of torment. She shuddered and turned the worship tape up even louder.

CHAPTER 33

I am sending you out like sheep among wolves. Therefore, be as
shrewd as snakes and as innocent as doves. ~Matthew 10:16 NIV

TAMARA AND HER BOYS MOVED INTO HER SISTER'S NEW RENTAL. THE
house was big enough to accommodate them all, although the boys
shared one room. Terri and Ray both worked fulltime, so Tamara's
interactions with them were limited.

Her new friend Tom continued to bring an element of the fun
she had long forgotten. He was taking her on little outings and
showing her a good time.

It felt good to laugh.

She loved the attention from Tom, but was determined not to
settle for the wrong guy.

Tom delighted Tamara with more insights of God and the Bible.
She was quite taken with him, and admired the way he received her
barbs with a great sense of humor. Her biting tongue usually
distanced most men.

She was tired of not trusting anyone, so she let her guard down; but still wondered, would God bring someone this soon?

Tom continued to call and regularly attended church with her and Sandy.

The days of having their friend Sandy in the mix were becoming fewer. Her friend warned her about spending too much time alone with Tom, but she had never dated in a healthy way and it was intoxicating!

Only one other problem, Tamara's sons did not like mom's new friend Tom.

At all.

After a while, it got her attention. She realized she had children who were still in intense pain and in need of her full attention. She did not want to hurt Tom, but knew the flirtation needed to end.

The next afternoon, after returning from a trip to the river with her boys, Tamara went into her room to change. Terri walked by and pushed the door open, "The widow who lives for pleasure is dead while she lives!"

Too stunned to even respond, Tamara shut the door. She was familiar with the passage of scripture her sister just launched at her, but she was already wanting to make things right regarding Tom. So why was God admonishing her through her sister?

Tamara felt the sword of her father. It was not the healing knife of a surgeon as the Bible's corrections were meant to be, this cut was to wound beyond repair.

～

TAMARA INVITED TOM FOR DINNER WHILE THE BOYS WERE AT THEIR Father's for the weekend, and Ray and Terri were out of town.

She was finishing up the last touches on dinner when the doorbell rang.

"Smells great." Tom walked through the door and pulled her close, gazing intently into her eyes.

"Food's going to get cold if we don't sit down." she said, pushing him away.

After dinner, Tom leaned in and kissed her.

She gave in to the passion she'd held back for so long, and became lost in his embrace. Knowing it would be their last time together touched a desperate part of her.

Perhaps I'm overreacting by ending the relationship so soon, she thought.

You must overcome the spirits in the man, not the man himself, God's whisper interrupted her thoughts.

"No Tom, we can't do this. I just had a Proverb come to me about a man taking fire into his bosom and thinking that his clothes will not be burned by it! I know what that means now, I feel fire in my chest! For the first time, I know what it's saying, we're going to get burned, we can't see each other anymore!"

"Tamara, I know that we struggle with lust for one another, but God showed me that the only way we can battle the temptation is to lay naked with each other, only then will we be free from fantasizing."

In a matter of seconds, her mind scrolled through the times she sensed red flags, but had chosen to ignore them.

Her resolve was back. She no longer had a tolerance for this so-called man of *god*.

As she saw him to the door her stomach ached. She wanted to throw up, she could not believe what a fool she'd been.

Have I learned nothing?

She crawled into bed and pulled the covers over her head wanting to die. *Are all men liars?*

King David had written that in the 116th Psalm. In his alarm he had thought so too.

After much repentance, Tamara made a vow to God. No more dating!

God would have to show her clearly whom He had for her.

A month later Tamara was called to testify about Tom's behavior before a church committee. He had pursued another Christian woman in the singles group and tried to take advantage of her as well. Shame came calling, once again.

Tamara was willing to humble herself, and go before the board for the sake of other women.

The day came and went, with no call to Tamara. The church held the meeting without her. She found out later that Tom charmed them. Deceiving them, he wiggled his way out of any real accountability and Tom soon moved on to another church.

Tamara cried, initially thankful she'd been spared humiliation, but her tears were more for the unsuspecting sheep of another fold. She wanted to warn them, to shout "Wolf!" from the rooftops. She knew that she had to surrender them to Jesus. He would love them perfectly and be their champion, just as He had been hers.

When God brought the man for her to marry, he would be a good and perfect gift to her and her sons.

She had to courageously face more lonely times as a single mother.

Tamara prayed to the Lord about whether she would be married again. She sensed that God was giving her a choice.

Tamara's thoughts went from her own loneliness and longing, to the needs of her sons for a father.

"Dear Lord Jesus, you've been such a good husband to me, but I'd like to be married again and have a godly man to help raise my sons unto you."

Immediately God prompted her to read from the book of Ruth. As she read about Boaz redeeming Ruth, she heard the still small voice of the Holy Spirit, "I have a Boaz for you."

Knowing that God was choosing a husband for her made Tamara weep.

"Will I have another child?" Tamara asked, right before she read the next part of the text, "So Boaz took Ruth and she became his wife. When he made love to her, the Lord enabled her to conceive, and she gave birth to a son." Ruth 4:13 (NIV)

The Lord's voice continued, "Who do you think put into your ex-husband's mind to stop your tubal ligation?"

Awe and wonder swept over Tamara. She recalled how bewildered she had been when she was 8 ½ months pregnant with her third child, and Brent decided he was going to get a vasectomy instead of her having her tubes tied.

"But Brent, it's already scheduled, once I have the baby it's a simple technique, I'm not afraid," Tamara said.

"I don't want you to go through that Tamara, we're cancelling it and I'm getting a vasectomy." replied Brent.

This was totally out of character for him, she could not believe he would even think of such an offer. It turned out; she was absolutely right.

The moment encompassed her. The Sovereignty of God left her completely undone. He was in control.

CHAPTER 34

BUT I SAID TO YOU, "YOU WILL POSSESS THEIR LAND; I WILL GIVE IT
to you as an inheritance, a land flowing with milk and honey." I am
the LORD your God, who has set you apart from the nations.
   ~ Leviticus 20:24 NIV

THE NEW START IN OREGON WAS EXHILARATING AT FIRST. TAMARA
had never been so free.

However, living with Terri's family became increasingly
uncomfortable. Ray and Terri started partying with their neighbors
on the weekends and Terri seemed to be leaving God behind.

One morning Terri asked Tamara out to breakfast. While
waiting for their food, Terri shared her exciting news. A big check
had come in from Ray's business and he was taking her and the girls
to Hawaii.

Tamara wanted to be genuinely happy for them, but that
familiar sickness rose up. Her sister was being bought off, and she
knew it.

The waitress plopped their piping hot plates in front of them,
and refilled their coffee.

"That is great Terri. So, your family counseling must be going well?"

"The girls told the counselor they made the whole thing up, that Ray never did anything to them." Terri responded calmly.

"What?" Tamara was incredulous. "Terri, you know that is a lie!"

Terri looked smugly at Tamara, "They said they made it all up because they heard your boys telling stories."

"But...you know that isn't true, Terri. The girls told their story *before* my boys talked about anything! Besides that, Anthony and I heard his confession on the phone. He finished Alicia's story!"

Terri laid aside her napkin, along with the truth. "We have a fresh start now. I'm putting all of this craziness behind us and moving on with Ray. He said he is sorry for the way he treated us in the past, and I can tell that he is changed."

Upon seeing her sister's choice to willingly go back under the spirit of deception, Tamara rose from the table, but had to steady herself. The room swirled before her.

Terri grabbed Tamara by the arm, and guided her to the front to pay. "We'll continue to help you and the boys; you can stay with us as long as you need."

Tamara nodded numbly in agreement. She had nowhere else to go.

Back at Ray and Terri's, Tamara looked in the newspaper for an apartment. She had to find a place for her and her children.

~

TUESDAY MORNING, TAMARA WENT TO THE CHURCH OFFICE AND asked about counseling. She was desperate to find out what to do next.

Within moments the church secretary was on the phone with one of their newest staff members. A beautiful middle-aged woman, exquisitely dressed, made her way towards Tamara. Her smile and warm embrace were just what Tamara needed.

"Hi, my name is Lavonna. I am so happy to meet you!"

She ushered Tamara back into her office and Tamara felt so comfortable, she gladly gushed forth the plight that she and her sons had endured.

Lavonna seemed quite taken with Tamara, and reassured her that she and her boys were safe now. *Finally*! Tamara sighed a breath of relief, someone who did not look at her like she was crazy or an unforgiving, bitter woman, refusing reconciliation with her family!

As Tamara left the office, she was too excited to pay attention to the uneasiness in the pit of her stomach. She brushed it off, and rejoiced in her newfound mentor.

She glanced down at the card that Lavonna gave her with her number and address. Lavonna was setting up a meeting with her very own apartment manager. They had an opening!

~

MOVING INTO THEIR NEW APARTMENT WAS A JOY. THE PLACE WAS perfect for a single mom with three sons. The boys hadn't finished bringing in the boxes, when a basketball rolled out of one.

"Mom, we'll be back soon. Promise!" They yelled as they dribbled the ball across the carpet.

The large basketball court was calling. Tamara didn't have the heart to scold them for bailing on the work.

She sat down in the middle of the mess, closed her eyes and thanked God.

~

ONCE THE INITIAL FUN WORE OFF OF THEIR NEW PLACE, ALL OF THE anger and fear long suppressed in her sons now bounced off her apartment walls.

"Brandon, you have to get up for school!" Tamara pleaded for the fifth time.

"Get away from me, you psycho!" he yelled.

Pulling the covers off only made her 16-year-old son more furious with her. He was skipping school frequently and hanging out all night with his new friends. Her once sweet and compliant little boy with beautiful brown eyes had been buried, underneath years of pain.

Tamara knew her younger boys would be next, following in his rebellious footsteps if something didn't give.

God was still good in the midst of the hardship. He met their needs, down to the smallest thing. Tamara secured a job as a hostess once her alimony ran out, but things remained tight.

Tamara put cereal out for the boys one morning and reached into the fridge for milk. "Empty." She sighed, swirling the tablespoon of milk left in the bottom of the jug.

They had no money, and payday wasn't for a few more days.

She removed the $1.39 coupon for milk from the refrigerator magnet and looked up. *Please Lord, my boys need milk.*

Midway through her morning shift, a customer approached her and pressed money into the palm of her hand.

"Oh. No sir," Tamara said to the kind man, "The tip is left on the table for the waitress and she gives me a portion once a week."

The man kindly responded, "I already gave the waitress her tip. This is for you personally."

As the gentleman walked away, Tamara counted the money; a wadded-up dollar bill and some change.

$1.39!

Through tears of joy, she made her way back to the break room to put the precious milk money into her purse.

She worshipped deeply in the midst of the hustle and bustle of the truck stop, transforming that restaurant breakroom into a sanctuary.

TAMARA'S LITTLE APARTMENT BECAME A GATHERING PLACE FOR HER children's friends. She embraced them all. Although feeding them became a challenge, she gladly shared what she could. Her job as a Hostess transitioned into waiting tables and the daily tips afforded them a little extra.

Aaron returned home from Brent's one evening with a little bundle in his arms. "Mom, can we keep him? Please? Dad's friend can't have him anymore so they gave him to me!"

Bijou, the cutest little Chinese Pug, initially brought more anxiety to Tamara. One more mouth to feed, along with vet appointments, and house training!

How could she turn down her son, so lit up with joy? "Okay Aaron, but you have to help with taking him out to the bathroom!"

"I will Mom. I promise! And he can sleep with me!" Aaron exclaimed. He whisked past her and into his bedroom with his new buddy!

Never had Tamara allowed a dog in her home. Until now.

Little did she know what a gift God had sent.

A WEEK LATER, TAMARA SAT EARLY IN THE MORNING APPLYING HER make-up at the counter in the little nook outside of the bathroom. Movement in the corner of her eye startled her. A quick assessment showed her that Aaron had shut the dog out of their room for snoring. She watched as Bijou stood up, circled, sat back down. Stood up, circled, and sat back down. The poor puppy could not get back to sleep.

"Bijou!" she cooed, scooping the puppy into her arms. "Did the boys kick you out of their bedroom again?"

She opened the boy's door and lay the sleepy dog down beside Aaron. Bijou circled once, snuggled into his master, and fell into a deep snore. *Wow, that was fast,* Tamara smiled.

As she finished getting ready for work, she heard her Lord's voice, *you too will only find rest in Your Master's presence.*

WHEN SCHOOL LET OUT FOR SUMMER, A BEAUTIFUL LITTLE HISPANIC girl named Mona started to follow Tamara and her sons to the swimming pool. Tamara noticed that she always swam in her shorts and a tank top, so she purchased a swimming suit, but knew she must wait for an opportune time when her gift could be received.

Mona's mother Maria was single, with several children, and spoke no English. Her children translated for her. Mid-summer, Maria started to trust Tamara and allowed her daughter to enter her apartment to color or have story time with Tamara's youngest son.

The anticipated day finally came, and Tamara put the package into Mona's hands.

Mona's big brown eyes widened with excitement, "What is it?"

"I guess you'll have to open it to see, Mona!"

Mona squealed with delight as she held up the bright red and pink swimsuit. Without another word, she turned on her heel and disappeared.

Twenty minutes later, she flew back through Tamara's front door in her new suit, holding out a tray covered with aluminum foil.

"These are from my Mama. She makes Tamales and she wants to thank you for my swimming suit." Mona smiled.

As Tamara put the Tamales into the refrigerator, Mona asked her a question that left her stunned.

"My Mama would like to know where you buy your Spanish Christian music."

Perplexed, Tamara responded; "Oh sweetie, I don't have any Spanish music."

"Oh yes! You do! We hear it coming out of your windows all of the time!"

Tamara was amazed. God had translated her Christian tapes into Spanish!

In the midst of so much pain, the beauty of her God swept in, in the most wondrous ways!

CHAPTER 35

And teach them to faithfully follow all that I have commanded you.
And never forget that I am with you, every day, even to the
completion of this age. ~Matthew 28:20 TPT

EXHAUSTED, TAMARA BROUGHT BACK THE FINAL LOAD OF CLOTHES
from the laundry room in the adjacent building. Folding her oldest
son's favorite Zumiez T shirt, she reflected on the hellish night.

"Brandon, you have a choice; to be in school or get a job. The
school is dropping you this week from the roster! The days of you
staying out all night, and me coming home from work to find our
food gone and the apartment trashed, are over!"

"You are such a witch! I hate you! You wrecked my life marrying
that jerk Brent!"

Brandon continued to scream profanities in his mother's face,
shoving her backwards.

"Stop yelling at Mom! Don't you *ever* touch her!" Aaron jumped
to his mother's defense.

The fight was on. Brandon's 6-foot frame towered over his little brother, but Aaron wasn't backing down. "I'll kill you!"

"Bring it on, you little punk!" yelled Brandon.

Puffing his chest out, Aaron went in for the tackle, while Joshua cried and Bijou barked.

Tamara intervened, "Nobody is killing anybody! Haven't you boys had enough of fighting? You are scaring your little brother!"

It was hard to pull Aaron off his older brother, "I know you are sticking up for me, but this is not the way!" she cried.

Brandon stormed out, slamming the door behind him. Aaron scooped his dog into his arms and headed to his room.

She never knew when Brandon might be back, but hoped it would be before her younger boys got off the bus the next day. She would be at work and needed Brandon to pick them up.

She chided herself for her thoughts going there first.

"Get ready for bed boys, it's already past your bedtime. I'll come in for prayers in a bit."

"Why do you serve Jesus Mommy?" Aaron asked. "He doesn't do anything for you."

Plopping on the end of his bed, she sobbed. "Oh Aaron, because Jesus is worthy of all of our praise. He saved us from going to Hell and if that is all He ever does, it is enough. I serve Him because He is worthy."

Aaron, seemingly satisfied with the answer, padded off to the bathroom and joined Joshua to brush his teeth.

Tamara was emotionally wrecked, and although she meant what she said to her son, she understood why he had asked her the question. It *was* as if God led them out and then disappeared.

She poured her heart out as she lay in the dark. *Please God, give me a sign, show me that you are with me. I can't go on without knowing I am on the right path. If I am deceived and out here on my own, then we won't make it. But if You are with me, I know we'll be fine!*

She fell asleep with new hope, anticipating God to awaken her with a sign.

The next morning Tamara woke up with a heavy heart.

She truly believed God was somehow going to reveal Himself to her in the night.

The familiar smell of freshly brewed coffee brought some normalcy to her bizarre world when she entered the truck stop. Suddenly her boss Lucy flew to greet her, something she had never done before. "Tamara, some old guy was looking for you this morning, he sat over there," she pointed to the counter. "He said he had a message for you."

Tamara's heart leapt, she *knew* this had to be the sign, "Lucy, what was the message?"

"Well, first he asked for you by name. When I told him you wouldn't be on shift for another hour, he said to give you a message; that you needed to know that God is with you. But I told him you already knew that."

Tamara had shared her faith with Lucy many times, so she did not get the significance of the message.

"But Lucy, you don't understand. I was crying out to God last night, asking Him for a sign!"

"The old guy *said* I didn't understand. That he had a word for you from the Lord; he repeated himself *strongly*, 'Tell Tamara that God is with her. She is on the right path and to *keep going*. God is with her!'

Tamara threw her arms around her boss, hugging and thanking her for delivering the blessed message.

"Lucy, God sent me an angel! I went to bed crying out to God for a sign last night. I've been having a really hard time and needed a reassuring word that I am on the right path with my sons!"

"Well Tamara, I don't think it was an angel. He looked pretty dirty and had an old crumpled up Bible. I think an angel would at least take a bath!" she laughed.

"Oh no, Lucy." Tamara replied, "That's *just* who God would send!"

Tamara never again doubted her decision in moving. God promised in His word that He'd set the lonely in families and she knew that her Boaz was out there. But how long until they'd meet?

CHAPTER 36

But solid food is for the mature, who by constant use have trained themselves to distinguish good from evil. ~Hebrews 5:14 NIV

ONE BALMY SATURDAY EVENING, TERRI CALLED. "WE'RE HAVING A little get together at the neighbors new pool for Alicia's birthday and we'd like the boys to come."

Tamara prayed in her spirit, but still couldn't discern whether or not to accept the invitation on her children's behalf. She longed for her family to be healed and restored in Jesus name, and each invitation to be with them was met with intense wrestling.

Tamara covered the mouthpiece of the phone, "Boys!"

Three heads turned from the Nintendo game, "What?"

"Do you want to go to Alicia's birthday party next week?"

Aaron responded first," Heck yeah Mom! Will there be pizza?"

"I don't know goofball, but I know they will have plenty of food!" said Tamara.

"No thanks." said Brandon.

"There's a huge pool Brandon, you would have fun too." she said.

"I want to go!" Joshua chimed in.

"I guess I'll go too." Brandon conceded.

Tamara moved her hand off the mouthpiece, "They all want to come, what time should I have them there?"

"Great! Bring them over around Four o'clock, and don't forget their towels." Terri chirped happily.

WHEN THE DAY CAME, TAMARA WALKED HER BOYS INTO THE backyard. Fun and festivities were in full force and the boys hurriedly jumped into the beautiful new pool.

"Jesus bless you and keep you." Tamara yelled over the commotion. They had become her parting words to her sons, each and every time they left her sight.

"Hey Tamara!" Terri called from the hot tub, holding up a frosty margarita. "Why don't you join us?"

"Oh, no thanks, I have to get going."

Ray yelled something over the music. Tamara couldn't quite make it out, but she was sure it was something to the effect of, "Little Miss Goody Two Shoes!"

As Tamara drove away, the usual conflicts arose. *What am I thinking? I should have never brought the boys over there!*

She had learned long before to cover her boys with prayer. But still, she berated herself for letting the boys decide. She knew if she went back now, her sons would be furious with her. They were innocent and simply wanted to swim with their cousins.

When she arrived home, the familiar tangible loneliness greeted her.

She sat down and cried. She had no one to call except Lavonna, and she was out for the evening. Bijou circled a few times at her feet, laid down and went into a full snore. She patted him.

There was a day that she would have relieved this feeling by going to a bar for a drink. She would have had company in no time.

Those days were over and now she sat alone, knowing that she could not escape this time of her life. She must go through it.

She reached for her Bible and came upon an obscure verse she had never read before,

"I never sat in the company of revelers, never made merry with them; I sat alone because your hand was on me and you had filled me with indignation." Jeremiah 15:17

Once again, the Word of the Lord tended her heart. It was the only place she found refuge. It had been hard to leave the laughter and fun and drive to an empty apartment, but if it was to be because God's hand was upon her, then she would submit and trust Him.

Around eleven pm the phone rang. "Mom, can you come? They're watching a scary movie. I want to come home!"

Tamara flew into the night cursing herself for being so stupid. She could hear the fear in Joshua's voice, and *she* had left him there!

After getting her sons into the car, Terri approached the vehicle.

"They were fine Tamara. You're making them into little wusses."

Tamara responded as lovingly as she could, "This is the kind of life that the Lord delivered us from Terri. We can't live like this anymore!"

Terri stood back from the car and with a look of utter disdain said, "This house will stand and there's nothing you can do about it!"

CHAPTER 37

ANYONE WHO LOVES THEIR FATHER OR MOTHER MORE THAN ME IS not worthy of me; anyone who loves their son or daughter more than me is not worthy of me. Whoever does not take up their cross and follow me is not worthy of me. Whoever finds their life will lose it, and whoever loses their life for my sake will find it.
~Matthew 10:37-39 NIV

TAMARA STRUGGLED WITH THE REALITY THAT SHE HAD NO CLOSURE as one has with the passing of loved ones. She had no funeral to attend, no family and friends gathering to comfort her in her loss. Her grieving was surreal, her family and friends still walked the earth, but they were still gone to her.

Losing most of her relationships by being uprooted from darkness felt as real as losing them through death. Neither did she have any sense or hope of reconciliation here, or in Heaven.

The passages in Hebrews 6:4-6 seemed a description of her once enlightened family.

"It is impossible for those who have once been enlightened, who have tasted the heavenly gift, who have shared in the Holy Spirit, who have tasted the goodness of the word of God and the powers of the coming age and who have fallen away, to be brought back to repentance. To their loss they are crucifying the Son of God all over again and subjecting him to public disgrace."

~

THE HOLY SCRIPTURES WERE BECOMING MORE AND MORE THE standard through which she processed everything.

One day as she sat listening to a teaching at a conference, a verse from the Song of Solomon was inscribed upon Tamara's heart.

The teacher explained how the Shulamite maiden had gone out into the streets, seeking the One whom her soul loved, and the watchman found her and beat her.

"The watchmen were to be the very guardians of her soul," she stated. "But they did not understand the Shulamite maiden and beat her with their incorrect counsel."

Tamara fell apart, searching blindly in her purse for a tissue.

That was it!

In her search for Jesus, she had been misunderstood, spiritually and emotionally beaten by counsel in the church. Her heart longed to find the One she loved, and follow Him completely.

After the meeting, Tamara regained her composure and approached the speaker, "Thank you!"

Tamara continued on with a few nonsensical sentences, trying once again to explain her plight and what this woman's teaching meant to her. After a few moments, she stopped, shame burning her cheeks.

A thank you would have sufficed.

The woman simply smiled and gave her a maternal hug.

It was enough.

~

THE CHURCH CONTINUALLY FAILED TO MEET THE EXPECTATIONS

that Tamara put upon it, yet she always forgave and went back. Many times, it was not even a matter of forgiveness, but a matter of lowering expectations or releasing the body of Christ altogether.

Her wounds were so deep, there was no congregation on earth that could have been wholly what she needed. The minute she heard a believer say she was like family, she believed her and her boys would be taken in. They would be safe and secure, established in a community of God.

When the Holidays came, she and her boys watched as families drove away after church to their parties and festive gatherings, while they drove home to their empty apartment.

On her first Christmas, she found herself broke. She had no money for toys for her children and no decorations.

The church brought a box of gifts wrapped for her kids and she was so grateful.

That is, until Christmas morning.

"WHAT IS THIS?" AARON ASKED.

The shiny paper had been ripped away, revealing a wooden box with faded lettering, reeking of mildew. The game was so old, it was unrecognizable; pulled from someone's attic, no doubt.

Joshua's shoulders sagged as he opened his gift. A toy car with half of the paint worn off, and a ragged Teddy bear for a child half his age.

Brandon held up a used shirt twice his size, "Figures!" he grumbled and threw it across the couch.

"Is this what we're worth? Used things?" The boys asked.

She tried to coax the boys into a thankful heart, but truthfully, she felt indignant herself.

Was that all the church felt they were worth?

In reality, a few older ladies had gathered what they could. They meant no harm in their offering.

There was no perfect church this side of Heaven.

She cried repentant tears that night, *Lord, I am so sorry for complaining, I am rich because I have you!*

She heard the Lord whisper, *Revelations 2:9.* She opened her Bible and read, "I know your afflictions and your poverty-yet you are rich." Rev 2:9

CHAPTER 38

Then the angel said to me, "Write this: Blessed are those who are invited to the wedding supper of the Lamb!" And he added, "These are the true words of God." ~ Revelation 19:9 NIV

SHE SPENT HER FIRST EASTER IN THE TOWN OF PLEASURE ALONE. Her youngest boys were with their Father for the weekend, and Brandon stayed with friends.

Tamara went up to the Chinese restaurant around the corner and placed an order to go. Upon entering her empty apartment, another wave of loneliness swept over her, threatening to suck her into an ocean of despair. She popped up for air, but then another wave hit.

As she sat down at the table to eat, her eyes landed on each chair where her sons usually sat, memories of past holidays haunting her.

She lifted her head to the only painting that hung in her stark dining room. The Lord's Last Supper.

Staring up at the face of Jesus, she wept silently and whispered, "Nobody wants to eat with me."

What happened next surpassed anything she had ever known. It was as if Jesus literally stood up and stepped out of the painting. His Presence filling the room, and seated Himself at the head of the table, "I want to eat with you."

Jesus spoke in the most tender voice that swept across her spirit. His Presence was tangible. "You are fellowshipping with my suffering, I too long for the day when all of my children will sit around my table and eat with me."

Tamara could not tell how long they sat there. There seemed to be no time, just she and her Lord in sweet communion.

WHEN THE BOYS RETURNED FROM THEIR FATHER, IT WAS ALWAYS A challenge. The steps they gained in healing always seemed to regress when they visited their dad. The fighting and screaming continually challenged the peace Tamara longed for.

She tried to calm down her boys, but was inevitably caught up into their chaos. Each time, she purposed to respond with patience, but many times succumbed to the pain in the atmosphere.

Her bedroom became her only sanctuary. Coming home from work each day she was depleted.

One afternoon, knowing that a long evening of caring for her sons lay ahead, she escaped to her room for at least a half an hour. She lay face down on the floor, pressing the button on her CD player to release the life-giving worship. It became a part of her routine, and was always enough for her to make it through until bedtime.

CHAPTER 39

Return to your rest, my soul,
for the LORD has been good to you.
For you, LORD, have delivered me from death,
my eyes from tears,
my feet from stumbling,
that I may walk before the LORD
in the land of the living. ~Psalm 116:7-9 NIV

A YEAR AFTER MOVING INTO HER APARTMENT, A BARRAGE OF DOUBTS
was launched by the age-old nemesis, Satan. *Did God really call you to
this place?*

It was a bright and beautiful first day of summer, so Tamara
packed a picnic lunch and loaded the bikes into the car. She
watched with happiness as her boys pedaled into the wooded area
of the park.

She relaxed on a blanket, settling in for a little Bible study, when
screams from her sons echoed out of the trees.

She ran as fast as she could, and was met halfway by two of her sons. They had ridden their bikes through a patch of stinging nettles, their legs and arms bright red.

Tamara's heart plummeted while she packed everything back up and went home. An oppression rolled over her, obscuring it seemed, even the sun. The rest of the day was filled with tears and more questions of God. Her belief that God was all good, seemed to be challenged.

The ongoing hits sometimes made her want to give up and die.

King David's words from the Psalms, reached a deeper place in her than her feelings.

"I will not die but live, and will proclaim what the Lord has done." Psalm 118:17

ROLLERBLADING BECAME THE BOY'S OBSESSION. TAMARA BORROWED roller blades and joined them.

Her first time out, she came to a slight hill. "Boys, I am not skating down this hill, I will walk down on the grass and meet you at the bottom."

They whizzed past her grinning and turned back just in time to see mom fall, sideways.

"Jesus!" Tamara screamed.

The pain from the snap in her leg was not the only reason she screamed; it was the realization that she had no insurance. Cynthia, the mother of one of her boys' friends, helped Tamara to her car.

Tamara insisted that she did not need to go to the Dr., trying to convince herself, more than Cynthia, that it was simply a sprain.

As the night wore on, it became obvious that Tamara needed medical attention.

Sure enough, she had broken her leg and the Dr. had to reset it, which was more painful than the initial break.

As she lay on the table, tears slid into her ears. *God, I can't afford time off work and the Dr. bills. What am I going to do?*

Six weeks off work followed. But miraculously, she made it through without losing their apartment.

WHILE IT WAS TRUE THAT GOD PROVIDED ALL OF TAMARA'S NEEDS, unexpected bills piled up. The bill collectors kept calling, and she fought off panic.

Then another bill arrived from the radiologist department. She tried to talk the billing department into lowering her monthly payments, but was met with indifference. "Ma'am, you have to pay us a minimum of fifty dollars per month or we will start garnishing your wages." The woman spoke curtly.

"Fifty dollars may not seem like much to you, but I am a single mom with three sons and barely make it as it is. Can you please accept a lower payment?" Tamara pleaded.

"No, fifty dollars is what you must pay each month."

Tamara rested the phone on her shoulder, her mind swimming, *where do I find an extra fifty?* She prayed to God for mercy.

The woman finally agreed to a smaller payment, but was still very rude and threatening. Tamara was rude back.

The rest of the day, the conversation convicted her. She knew what the Holy Spirit was telling her to do.

She called the number the next morning and spoke with the bill collector. "Hi. This is Tamara Sawyer, we spoke on the phone yesterday."

"Can I help you with something further?" The woman asked.

"No, I actually called to apologize for my attitude. You did not deserve that. You were simply doing your job and I should not have been rude. Please forgive me."

Tamara's statement was met with a long silence.

"I have never had an apology in all the years I have worked here. I don't even know what to say." The woman finally responded.

"You don't need to say anything. Keep up the good work, and have a wonderful day." Tamara said.

"Well, thank you. Thank you so much, you made my day!" she said.

As Tamara hung up the phone, she sat in awe of God and His ways, that were indeed higher than hers.

TAMARA TRIED TO STAND STRONG, BUT SOMETIMES SHE COULDN'T
shake unbelief. Trial upon trial rocked her. One morning she asked
God to once again reassure her that moving to this town was the
right thing.

She clearly heard His response in her spirit, *go to the library and
look up Pleasure's roots.*

While the boys shot hoops at the basketball court, Tamara drove
to the local library. She found the History section and scanned the
rows of books.

One book in particular caught her eye. It was a thin, green
hardback book.

She pulled it off the shelf and found a comfy chair in the corner
of the library. After reading the first few pages, she sat up, stunned.
The book recounted how the early settlers walked along dirt roads
praying, and nicknamed their beautiful town *The garden of Eden.*

God had led her out of her hometown with the Scripture from
Joel 2:3

"Before them the land is like the garden of Eden, behind them,
a desert waste---"

THAT EVENING, AS SHE DRIFTED OFF TO SLEEP, THE LORD WHISPERED
into her soul, *Bind the spirit of death.*

A bit alarmed, she prayed aloud, "I bind the spirit of death, in
Jesus name!"

Tamara felt as if her heart might beat out of her chest. *Why did
God ask me to pray that?*

In the morning when she awakened her sons for school, she saw
that the long cord of Joshua's nightstand lamp was wrapped around
his neck!

"Jesus!" she cried, hysterically unwrapping the black tentacles.
At least six times she uncoiled the cord, uncovering the whole length
of her son's neck.

She held him, sobbing, "Joshua, the lamp somehow came unplugged and wrapped around your neck in the night. Are you okay? Does your throat hurt?"

"I'm okay mom, can I get some cereal?"

He was going to be okay, but the responsibility of prayer was more evident than it had ever been. It left her trembling.

CHAPTER 40

But when you fast, put oil on your head and wash your face, so that
it will not be obvious to men that you are fasting, but only to your
Father who is unseen; and your Father, who sees what is done in
secret, will reward you. ~ Matthew 6:16-18 NIV

GOD CALLED TAMARA TO FAST FOR THREE DAYS MANY TIMES
throughout her journey of deliverance and it was never easy; but
this third day of her fast was particularly taxing. The smell of bacon
wafted over her as she hung up her jacket in the break room.
Delivering her first order of piping hot omelets oozing with cheese
to a table was pure torture.

"God, I have to work, I just need some toast!" she whispered,
grabbing a piece that had been long abandoned under the heat
lamps. The much-anticipated morsel turned to dust in her mouth.
She spit it out, and surrendered once again to fasting.

The next day she got a phone call from her sister Terri. "Hey
Tamara, I got a call from Mom. She spent all day yesterday in
prayer for you. She thinks you are deceived and that you need to be

back with the family. She also said Dad is at the end of his rope, that he is even desperate enough to kidnap you."

"I'm never going back Terri, and I refuse to live in fear of Mom and Dad."

"Yeah, I know." Terri responded.

Tamara knew why she had been fasting, her obedience had somehow thwarted the demonic intercession of her mother and the plans of her father.

Later that afternoon, while shopping at the grocery store, Tamara became overwhelmed with the realization that her sons did not have a godly role model in their lives; not one man.

How will they get through this world? How will they know how to walk the earth as sons of God?

Spiraling into despondency, she heard God's voice thunder into her soul, *"I Myself will shape and hone your sons!"*

It snapped her immediately out of her self-pity, and back into the reality of finishing her shopping for three hungry boys.

That evening, exhausted after another long and emotional day, she opened her Bible:

"All your sons will be taught of the LORD; And the well-being of your sons will be great." Isaiah 54:13

She held the precious book to her breast, as the Heavenly Father transcribed it onto the tablet of her heart.

CHAPTER 41

When tempted, no one should say, "God is tempting me." For God cannot be tempted by evil, nor does he tempt anyone; but each person is tempted when they are dragged away by their own evil desire and enticed. Then after desire has conceived, it gives birth to sin; and sin, when it is full grown gives birth to death. Don't be deceived my dear brothers and sisters. Every good and perfect gift is from above, coming down from the Father of the heavenly lights, who does not change like shifting shadows. ~James 1:13-17 NIV

THERE WAS AN UNMISTAKABLE CHARISMA ABOUT HIM. HE HAD THE presence of a TV Evangelist, handsome, immaculately groomed, in a suit cut from the finest cloth.

Lavonna steered him through the after-service church crowd, "Tamara, I'd like you to meet Grayson."

"Hi Grayson, nice to meet you."

The exchange was brief and Tamara thought no more of it. Grayson was a nice older man, at least twenty years her senior. It seemed obvious to her that he and Lavonna were a perfect couple.

On a walk through the neighborhood one warm evening, Lavonna inquired about Tamara's love life. "Do you have your eye on anyone? You are such a beautiful woman Tamara, I bet men are lined up to date you. I need to protect you."

"No, not yet. It will have to be someone special though. Having three boys scares most men off. But I know God has promised a Boaz for me one day." said Tamara.

Lavonna got very quiet, "I wonder if it's Grayson."

Tamara stopped and turned to Lavonna, "Of course it's not! Why would you even say that? I see him with *you*!"

"Oh honey, I'm being silly. Are you going to the women's retreat this year? If you are, let's spend time together!" Lavonna said.

"I don't think I can afford it this year, but we'll see."

Tamara still had a hard time shaking off the strange comment. Lavonna had shared with her before how crazy she was about the man, and hoped to marry him.

A few nights later Tamara awoke from a deep sleep. A large TV screen appeared above her bed, framed with dazzling colors. A man's face appeared, fuzzy at first, but when she could distinguish the features, it was Grayson! "Tamara, I am your husband."

The vision ended.

Unable to get back to sleep, Tamara arose from her bed. She was shaken and confused. Was that a vision from God or Satan? Perhaps Lavonna was prophetic, planting a selfless seed, or had the enemy planted a seed that was now being watered by a false vision?

No answer came that night.

As Tamara pondered the vision, over the next few weeks, Grayson frequently showed up near her or drove past her house. Uncanny coincidences kept happening. Her thoughts went to the sketch of Boaz, a good man in the Old Testament, who redeemed a woman named Ruth from a destitute life. He was many years Ruth's senior, a wealthy man of God. Could Lavonna have been correct? Was Grayson her Boaz? She finally decided that Grayson was to be Lavonna's intended, and laid all other scenarios to rest.

Within a few weeks of her decision to not think about her Boaz, Lavonna asked Tamara to assist Grayson's daughter Janet in leading a women's Bible study. Tamara agreed without a thought. She loved Bible studies and helping women to grow in their walk with Christ.

Lavonna invited Tamara and Janet over for tea so they could meet. Janet walked right into Tamara's heart! She thought she was the most adorable woman she had ever seen, with brunette hair and big beautiful brown eyes. It was not just her cuteness that drew out Tamara's maternal instincts, but something more. Tamara wanted to somehow help her, and not just with the Bible study. Janet was like a lost little girl and Tamara wanted to help her find her way home.

After spending time with Janet, Tamara felt a check in her spirit, an uneasiness about Lavonna putting her in a lead position of a Bible study. It was clear that Janet was very young in her faith and knowledge of the Bible.

~

THE FIRST BIBLE STUDY TOOK PLACE AT STACY'S HOME. STACY WAS another newly divorced woman whom Lavonna had taken under her wing. Quick witted and charming, Tamara took a liking to Stacy immediately.

The ladies also shared a mutual admiration of Lavonna. The study was a group of divorcees,' wounded women gathering for comfort and growth in Christ.

The evening began effortlessly, with introductions and refreshments. However, Tamara could see that Janet was still nervous. Her hands trembled as she handed out copies from a book she'd found at her mother's house.

Then she began to share some *insights* from the book.

Tamara froze as she read the paper. It was not Christian at all. It was from a mystical book of New Age teachings. Janet's mother Sharon had been in a solid Bible teaching church all her life, so Janet had not questioned the books content.

Tamara looked around the room and saw the other women squirming. She prayed silently, asking God for wisdom, she knew she

something, yet she did not want to shame this innocent
an of God.

can I speak with you in private?" asked Tamara,
temporarily pausing the study.

They stepped out onto the front porch, and as graciously as she
could, Tamara pointed out the New Age content of the paper.

Devastation washed over Janet's face. "I'm so sorry. I didn't
know!"

"Oh Janet, I realize that. I know your heart is pure, you are just
not ready to lead yet. It is not your fault!"

"I'm too embarrassed to go back in the house." Janet said.

Tamara wrapped her arms around her new friend and prayed
against shame. "I'll do the talking Janet, the women will
understand."

Stacy met them with a box of tissues when they stepped back
inside.

"Thank you," Janet cried. "I am so sorry you guys. Please
forgive me. I did not mean to give you anything New Age!"

The women reassured her that they did understand. Tamara
gathered all of the copies and ripped them in half. "This is a good
lesson for all of us on how careful we must be with what we read
and take in. If it does not line up with the Bible, we have to throw it
out."

"Yes," Stacy chimed in. "This is why we have Bible studies, right
ladies?"

Tamara tried to process it all on the drive home. She was not
upset with Janet, but angry with Lavonna for putting this woman in
a position of leadership for which she was clearly not ready.

Janet resigned as the leader that same evening, but signed on for
a lifelong friendship with Tamara.

CHAPTER 42

Nevertheless, I have this against you: You tolerate that woman
Jezebel, who calls herself a prophet. By her teaching she misleads
my servants into sexual immorality and the eating of food sacrificed
to idols. ~ Revelations 2:20 NIV

DESPITE THE SITUATION WITH JANET, TAMARA CONTINUED HER
counseling with Lavonna. Lavonna invited Tamara into her home
for personal visits and dinner parties. They were growing close, and
Lavonna introduced her to a couple of single men, seemingly
anxious to find her a husband. She confided in Tamara that
Grayson made it clear that he would never marry again.

Tamara adored Lavonna and became even more comfortable
with her, until one day, when Aaron rode his bike to the door and
asked to see his mom.

Lavonna snapped angrily at him, "Your mother is here for a
visit! You need to let her be!"

She shut the screen door in his face, then turned to Tamara,

ـly dripping from her lips, "Your boys need to let their ـ alone time."

ᴛamara was shocked at Lavonna's response to her son. Lavonna had previously told her boys to call her Grandma!

Lavonna obviously picking up on Tamara's distress, hustled toward her cookie jar and rushed to the screen door and offered Aaron a cookie.

Tamara rose from the couch, politely excused herself and walked home with her mind swirling.

Something was off, but what?

Aaron threw down his bike and followed his mother into their apartment, "Mom, that lady's a witch like Grandma!"

"Aaron! That is not true! Lavonna has been a great help to us. You need to be respectful!"

Tamara left the room but her sons words echoed in her soul.

~

ᴛᴀᴍᴀʀᴀ ᴀɴᴅ ᴛʜᴇ ʙᴏʏs ʟᴏᴠᴇᴅ ɢᴏɪɴɢ ᴛᴏ ᴄʜᴜʀᴄʜ. Iᴛ ᴡᴀs sᴏ different from anything they'd attended before. The church was held in a huge auditorium, electric with excitement and anticipation. The Pastor spoke of his love for his daughter, and it brought tears, as she longed for that kind of fatherly love.

During one service in particular, she thought to herself, *I wish I had a rapport with him.*

She heard the still small voice of the Holy Spirit.

That's Me Tamara, you have that rapport with Me. It's My Father's heart in him that you are sensing.

~

ᴛᴀᴍᴀʀᴀ ᴊᴏɪɴᴇᴅ ᴛʜᴇ ᴡᴏᴍᴇɴ's Bɪʙʟᴇ sᴛᴜᴅɪᴇs ᴀɴᴅ ᴍᴇᴛ sᴏᴍᴇ wonderful ladies. She studied the Word of God and treasured His promises of a better life for her and her sons. It never ceased to amaze her.

Lavonna seemed to get busier and busier and did not have much time for Tamara.

When Tamara did spend time with her, she went away shaking her head in confusion. Lavonna coarsely jested and talked about wanting to get drunk and have sex. She never seemed to manifest the fruit of the spirit in private. Lavonna had such a charisma onstage at church, that she practically glowed!

In the meantime, Tamara encountered another woman in the church named Elaine. She loved hearing Elaine's heart when she spoke at women's events, but there was always a wall between them.

Over coffee one afternoon, Tamara shared with Lavonna how much she had enjoyed Elaine's teaching.

"I would be careful, Tamara." said Lavonna.

"What? Why?"

"Elaine and Sonia have a problem with me. They are jealous in fact, and are out to ruin me." said Lavonna.

"Really? They seem so nice." Tamara said.

Sonia was another leader in the church and headed a thriving ministry. Tamara felt frustrated, there were so many women she admired, who spoke beautiful truths about God, but who could really be trusted?

~

A FEW NIGHTS LATER, TAMARA RECEIVED A CALL FROM LAVONNA. "Hi honey, I was hoping to ask you a small favor."

"Sure, what do you need?" responded Tamara.

"Well, you know how I shared about the women who have been questioning my staff position?"

"Are you referring to Elaine and Sonia?" Tamara asked.

"Yes. I need you to write a letter on my behalf, how you have witnessed my good character. The Pastor is calling a staff meeting to stop their attack."

"Of course, I will!" Tamara agreed.

"Thank you. You are such a gift to me; I don't know what I would do without you standing with me." she sniffed.

"Don't cry Lavonna, you know that God is for you!" Tamara said.

Tamara hung up the phone and grabbed a pen and paper, ready to help her friend. An hour or two went by and she still found herself scribbling and erasing. Nothing would flow.

Putting on her pajamas, she sat cross legged on the bed, notebook on her lap. Still, nothing. She went to sleep around midnight, exasperated. She did, after all, love this woman, and wanted to defend her from attack.

At two am she was awakened by the Lord. It was as if life since meeting Lavonna, flashed in front of her eyes. God reminded her of some of the times she ignored the red flags.

～

Lavonna told you to do what?" Tamara asked Stacy.

"She told me to send a rusty knife with 'Bobbitt' carved on the handle to my ex-husband!" Stacy repeated, laughing hysterically.

"That is so disgusting Stacy, I can't believe Lavonna told you to do that!" said Tamara.

The story had made all of the headlines about a disgruntled woman castrating her husband, and Tamara could find no humor in a Christian counselor suggesting such a thing to Stacy!

～

"Lavonna, I love it!" Tamara gushed.

Lavonna was officially a full-time staff member, and had been given a new office. She invited Stacy and Tamara in to see it. Lavonna, with mincing steps, paraded around her desk, and let out a loud cackling sound.

"Lavonna, you sound just like a witch!" Stacy gasped.

Startled, Tamara was speechless, that was exactly how she sounded.

Unphased at the comment, Lavonna continued the tour.

ALONG WITH RECOUNTING THE RED FLAGS, THE HOLY SPIRIT GUIDED Tamara through Scripture, exposing Lavonna. She could no longer deny that Lavonna was like her mother Victoria, just as Aaron had discerned.

At four o'clock in the morning, Tamara felt a nudge from the Lord to call Elaine.

"But God, it's four a.m. and I barely know the woman!"

He persisted, so she picked up the phone. After three rings Elaine groggily answered. Tamara barely stopped between breaths, telling Elaine all that she had seen, and how Lavonna had snuck into the camp.

Elaine paused after Tamara recited the verses, starting with Joshua chapter nine where the Gibeonite people deceived Joshua and the Israelite's into making a covenant with them. They were deceived because they had not sought the counsel of the Lord.

"Tamara, I have to be honest. I was suspicious of you when you first called because of your friendship with Lavonna, but the verses you quoted are the exact same scriptures that God gave me about the way Lavonna came onto our staff." Elaine said.

"So, what do I do now?" asked Tamara.

"Pray Tamara, in hopes that Lavonna will repent, and that truth be revealed. Then we simply trust God with the outcome."

ONCE TAMARA TOLD LAVONNA SHE COULD NOT DO AS SHE ASKED IN writing the letter, Tamara was banished from her favor.

"I am sorry that I can't write the letter, I spoke with Elaine and she wants this all to be resolved, she wants good for you Lavonna!"

"So, she has gotten to you too!" Lavonna barked.

"Lavonna, you know I love you." said Tamara.

"I have to get to a meeting." Lavonna coldly ended the conversation.

Tamara's fear of the Jezebel spirit initially squelched her desire to have anything to do further with Lavonna, but God's love compelled her on, to contend for her freedom in prayer.

Elaine invited Tamara to join her prayer group and they became friends. Tamara prayed and fasted for Lavonna.

God gave Tamara a prophetic word for her, an invitation into healing and restoration.

~

THE THIRD DAY OF HER FAST, TAMARA KNOCKED ON LAVONNA'S door.

"What do you want?" Lavonna asked, stone-faced.

"Lavonna, can I come in? I believe I am to share a word for you from God."

"Absolutely not! Never come to my door again!"

"Please Lavonna, just hear me out." cried Tamara.

Lavonna slammed the door in Tamara's face.

The next day, Elaine called Tamara. "Hi Tamara, I am sad to report that the meeting with the Pastor did not go like we'd hoped. He admonished Sonia and I and made us apologize to Lavonna for making her feel uncomfortable. We submitted to his authority and did as he asked, but he is still not seeing the truth about her."

"I don't understand Elaine, you and Sonia have been faithfully serving here for years, and Lavonna has only been here one year!" said Tamara.

"I know, but we continue to trust God and pray! And another thing, after our meeting, we went into the staff meeting and Lavonna announced to everyone that you have been stalking her, and that you are a witch."

"What?" Tamara asked, flabbergasted.

"Did you go to her house last night?" asked Elaine.

"Well, yes. But stalk her? Absolutely not! She actually accused *me* of being a witch?"

"I knew that you weren't stalking her, and you know that the Jezebel spirit is from the accuser, Satan. Lavonna also said that you banged on her windows and doors for three days shouting at her to let her in. You didn't do that, did you?"

"Of course not Elaine!" Tamara said.

"I didn't think so, but had to ask."

Nothing came of the meeting, and with everything swept under the rug, all went on as usual at church. Lavonna sat smugly in the reserved section of honor in the front.

Tamara's character was now the one in question.

CHAPTER 43

Praise be to the God and Father of our LORD Jesus Christ, the
Father of compassion and the God of all comfort, who comforts us
in all our troubles, so that we can comfort those in any trouble with
the comfort we ourselves receive from God.
~ 2 Corinthians 1:3-4 NIV

THE KNOCK AT THE DOOR CAME AS A SURPRISE. IT WAS 10 PM AND
nobody she knew would call at that hour.

"I punched him in the face!" Janet sobbed; hair plastered on her
face from the pelting rain.

"Oh sweetie, come in!" Tamara said. "Tell me what happened!
Who did you punch?"

"My husband Dusty, he has a horrible temper. He kept pushing
and hitting me! I couldn't take it anymore, so I punched him right in
the nose!" cried Janet.

"You are staying with me tonight. I have extra blankets and this
couch is pretty comfy. We will figure out next steps for you
tomorrow!" said Tamara.

Janet agreed.

One night turned into a month.

Hearing about Janet's marriage was hauntingly familiar. Tamara had an epiphany. Her own suffering was not to be in vain. Everything God had taught her she would gladly pour into her friend.

She awakened Janet each morning with a new scripture and it was turning her own mourning into joy!

A few weeks later, over coffee, Janet asked Tamara for more guidance. "What should I do? What is God saying? Can you get another scripture for me?"

Smiling at her hungry friend, Tamara tenderly responded, "It's time for you to ask Him yourself Janet. He is your Father too!"

Twenty minutes later Janet rushed to the vanity where Tamara stood doing her hair, "Tamara! God talked to me! He gave me a scripture!"

They both knew she had turned a corner, and would never be the same.

～

"It's too soon to go back Janet." said Tamara.

"I have to Tamara. I know Dusty is sorry. He will change, I just know it!" said Janet.

"I want to believe that too Janet. I know God can change hearts, but you need to be wise." Tamara forced a smile at her friend, although the pit of her stomach ached.

Dusty began regularly attending church and started counseling. Tamara hung out with the couple, and became strangely comfortable around Dusty. He was from the South like her dad. The Tennessee Confederate flag hung proudly in their family room, just like Tamara's dad's. They even had some of the same mannerisms and speech, referring to God as "The Good Lord."

Maybe God is showing me that men like my dad can be saved, Tamara thought.

Dusty generously offered to take the girls to a steak dinner one evening. The girls chatted excitedly about what God had been showing them in the Bible.

"So, what has God been doing in your life Dusty?" Tamara asked.

"Oh Tamara, you know I ain't no saint, just a mean ol' sinner saved by grace!" Dusty grinned.

The ladies laughed as Dusty told an off-color joke about Saint Peter.

Tamara's mirth was soon interrupted by a check within her spirit.

Do not sit at death's table again.

The comfort she'd been receiving from Dusty was not from the source of life, but from a spirit of death.

She'd only been in Janet's life a few short months, but saw clearly the familiar spirits that once ensnared her operating full scale in her friend's home.

Tamara interceded for her friend but did not know how to share her discernment. It was nothing she could prove. Past experience told her that nobody would believe her without proof.

It was only a matter of time before Dusty called. "Come get the lying witch, I want her out of my house!"

"I'm coming, Dusty. Don't you dare lay one finger on her! I will be right there!"

Tamara practically flew to her friend's home, praying as fast as she drove.

Dusty opened after the first knock, red faced and nostrils flaring.

"Where is she?" Tamara pushed past him into the house.

"She's in there!" He pointed.

Janet sat cowering in a corner of the bedroom, knees tucked into her chest visibly shaking and crying, obviously from being beaten. She couldn't speak, but her eyes, full of fear, desperately searched Tamara's face.

Tamara prayed and bound demonic spirits. Dusty entered the room and stepped in between them. "You're not taking her anywhere!"

Tamara was not leaving that house without her friend. A

boldness rose up within her.

"Dusty, I'm calling the police if you do not let us leave. You told me to come and get her, and I am not leaving without her!"

"Take the whore." Dusty growled through gritted teeth.

Tamara helped Janet up, shielding her with her own body and moving past Dusty as he yelled, "Don't bother coming back Janet! We're through!"

Dusty followed closely on their heels to the car. Tamara pulled away just as he reached for Janet's door handle.

Turning her head back, Janet watched him disappear around the corner, and muttered her first words, "It was my fault. I shouldn't have said what I said to him."

"I don't care what you said to him Janet. There is never a reason or excuse to hit a woman!"

~

At midnight, loud pounding, followed by a string of profanities woke Tamara up.

"Dusty, I called 911. You better leave! Janet is not going to talk to you!"

"Please, just let me see my wife! I love her! I'm so sorry for waking you up." he said, voice softening.

"Are you kidding me right now? You were just freaking out, I am not opening this door, now go away!"

Dusty pounded the door a few more times, "F--- You Tamara! You can't keep my wife away from me!"

When the police arrived, they wrote down the information and talked to Janet about seeking a restraining order.

She was not ready.

~

It would take months of prayer and seeking the truth before Janet realized she did not have to live like that ever again. She filed for a divorce and moved into an apartment.

The day finally came. Janet, her mother and Tamara walked into the county courthouse.

"Pray for me, Tamara," Janet asked.

Tamara grasped her friends shaking hands, "Heavenly Father, we thank you for your perfect peace, and your deliverance. Please give Janet the strength to see this through, in Jesus' name, Amen."

Janet's mother Sharon winked at Tamara. "Thank you," she whispered, "I don't think my daughter would have ever gotten free of Dusty without your friendship."

As Dusty walked into the room, Janet sighed deeply and grabbed Tamara's hand.

"You can do this Janet. Jesus is with you!" Tamara whispered.

Janet and Dusty walked into the Judge's chambers and the door closed behind them.

Half an hour later, the couple emerged, and somberly walked their separate ways. Tamara and Sharon pulled Janet into a group hug.

They quietly walked out of the building and into the park directly behind the courthouse. Tamara was bursting with anticipation. "How did it go in there? Are you okay?"

"Dusty pleaded with me and begged me to tear up the papers, I didn't respond. I just told the Judge that our marriage was beyond repair, and signed the final papers. And, to be honest, I'm actually better than okay, I'm free!"

Janet spontaneously let out a squeal, and climbed a children's elephant slide, slid down, and landed in the dirt, in her new dress.

They all three laughed as they helped her up.

"Time to celebrate. We are going to a fancy lunch on me!" Sharon said.

Dusty passed by as they drove out of the courthouse parking lot. Tamara saw Janet's gaze meet his. "He looks so sad!" Janet said.

"Don't go there Janet, he will suck you back in!" Tamara warned.

She knew a battle had been won, but a war was still on in the heavenlies.

God, only you can keep her free...

~

THE CLOSER JANET AND TAMARA GOT; THE MORE TAMARA FELT LIKE they were family. She wondered if Grayson was indeed her Boaz.

Tamara got a couple movies, some snacks and headed over to Janet's new apartment.

After the first movie, Tamara started an awkward conversation. "Janet, I need to talk to you about something and I'm so afraid that you are not going to understand."

Janet, looked a bit startled and set down the tortilla chip she had just dipped in salsa. "Tamara, I don't know what you need to tell me but I'm here for you. You can tell me anything."

"Okay. You know how I told you about God having a Boaz for me?" Tamara asked.

"Yeah, I remember." said Janet.

"Well, I think it might be your father, but I want you to know that our friendship has nothing to do with him! I wanted to get to know you long before I had an inkling that Grayson could be the man God spoke of. Please believe me!"

Janet lit up a cigarette and said, "Is that all? You're too good for him. You don't want to marry him and besides, he's a narcissist!"

Tamara was shocked, she was so used to being misunderstood. They talked, laughed and cried into the wee hours of the morning.

~

TAMARA DECIDED TO BE PROACTIVE LIKE RUTH OF THE BIBLE, BY going into Boaz's fields to glean. She began to strike up conversations with Grayson whenever she saw him. He was flattered with Tamara's attention and asked her out to dinner.

The wait staff acted as though a foreign dignitary had entered the restaurant. "Grayson, sir, so nice to see you again! What table would you like this evening?"

"Where would you like to sit Tamara?" Grayson asked.

"That table would be fine over there," she pointed.

"No, I don't like it; too close to the kitchen. We'll take that one," Grayson motioned to the Host.

"This is a nice place Grayson." Tamara said, still a bit embarrassed at her wrong choice of tables. "Thank you."

"You're welcome Tamara, you get a good deal here." said Grayson.

The waitress politely took their order and soon returned with their salads.

"Wow. That was fast." said Tamara.

"Yes, but I don't like it. Look at all that iceberg lettuce."

"Young lady," he motioned the waitress back to the table.

"Yes sir?" she asked.

"Take this excuse for a salad back to the kitchen. There is no nutritional value here. Find me some dark green lettuce!" Grayson snapped.

"Mine is fine." Tamara told the waitress as she attempted to remove her salad plate.

"So, Tamara, tell me a little about yourself; how you came to live in Pleasure."

"My story is pretty crazy. You probably don't really want to know. I just went through a horrible divorce and through God's grace, I am starting over here with my three boys." she said.

"Oh, my. That sounds rough. I went through a divorce years ago and love being single. I would never bite that bullet again." He grimaced.

Tamara took a long drink of her ice water.

Either I am way off on him being Boaz or we have a long way to go!

The drive home with Grayson was quiet. As he pulled into her driveway, he leaned over and gave her a brotherly hug. "Tonight was nice Tamara, I was feeling kind of lonely, so thank you."

"Thank you, Grayson. Call me sometime."

"Yeah, or I'll see you at church."

～

Tamara chose to call Grayson again. She convinced herself that he was just with the wrong women before, as she had been with the wrong man, so he was afraid of remarrying. If God was in it, Grayson would see their future together.

"Hi Grayson. There is a new movie out, would you like to see it with me?"

"Well sure, I don't have anything going on. Meet me at my house, I will drive." he said.

From that night on, they talked on the phone or hung out together. As the months went on, he began to make her feel beautiful. His charming words made her believe he was falling in love with her.

The more time they spent together, the more she saw how wounded and lonely he truly was.

"Grayson, it's late, I need to hang up now, I have to get up for my early shift at the restaurant."

"Come on Tamara, your voice always soothes me to sleep. You bring me such peace." he said.

"Why don't you try reading the Psalms? It always brings me peace." she said.

"Why don't you read one to me?"

She was so disappointed. She thought her Boaz would lead her spiritually. Once again, she was doing all the work in a relationship.

But she was up for it. She knew well how to love without getting anything in return.

She continued to pursue him with the love of God, writing him beautiful poems and surprising him with little gifts. He'd made it very clear from the start that he was a confirmed bachelor and did not want to raise her kids, but that did not dissuade her.

If God was in this, it would happen. They just needed more time.

One night as they were talking on the phone, Grayson was particularly vulnerable. "Tamara, pack your bag, right now. Come over and we can fly to Vegas, we'll get married!"

"You don't really mean that Grayson, you are lonely and in a moment of weakness." Tamara said.

"I guess you're right. I do love you and I would marry you in a heartbeat if you didn't have children. I already raised my kids and have no interest in raising anymore." said Grayson.

Tamara's heart sank as reality took hold and jerked her out of her fantasy. It was clear. If Grayson loved her, he would love her sons. She had an insight to God's heart in that moment, how He must ache as people professed their love to Him, but did not love His children.

She felt sick, realizing she had wasted time pursuing a man who could not possibly reciprocate her love.

The next morning Grayson called and thanked Tamara for not accepting his proposal.

"You are very welcome Grayson." Tamara responded coolly.

"So, are you busy tonight?" asked Grayson. "I thought we could grab a bite to eat together."

"Are you kidding me?" asked Tamara.

"No. Why would I be kidding? I already miss you and thought we could just go on as usual."

"Grayson, if I continue to see you, I will not meet the man God has for me. We can't see each other anymore."

She hung up the phone, and that chapter in her life was over.

Janet and Tamara remained best friends and Grayson asked about Tamara from time to time. He told Janet that he had been touched by God's love through her, and he missed it. Tamara was tired of being in charge of a man's happiness, period. She knew the sin that beset her, making men into idols, but had not realized she also let men make her into one.

It was sad to Tamara, Grayson was in a leadership position in the church, yet did not know the first thing about a true, intimate walk with Jesus.

Tamara erected a wall as tall as the Empire State Building to keep men away from her and her children.

CHAPTER 44

Turn to me and be gracious to me for I am lonely and afflicted.
~ Psalm 25:16 NIV

THE SINGLE LIFE BROUGHT A MIX OF RELIEF AND LONELINESS TO
Tamara. It felt great to not be controlled by someone, but not
having someone, could also be very lonely. No matter what state her
emotions were in, she loved to reach out to comfort and help others.

Hannah lived a few apartment doors down from her. She was a
newlywed and in need of some basic home making skills. Tamara
became her go to for all of her questions, not just about cooking,
but about life in general.

The young woman's past was filled with abuse, and she suffered
from night terrors. Tamara led her through healing prayers and
taught her things of the Bible.

"I haven't had another nightmare since you prayed over me
Tamara." Hannah shared.

"Praise God, Hannah, that is awesome!"

"So why does God allow pain in the first place?" she asked.

As soon as God would answer one prayer, another question of His goodness would come. For Hannah, and Tamara.

"Man has free will Hannah, and we are in a fallen world. Satan wreaks havoc, but God sent Jesus to destroy his works. I don't have a simple answer for you. We just need to have faith and trust that He is good. But, right now, I need to run over to the strip mall to take Bijou for a flea dip. Would you like to come with me? We can get a coffee afterward and chat some more."

"Sure. Let me lock up my apartment. I will be right back." said Hannah.

They took the shortcut behind their complex, and came to the small hill lined with thick, tall shrubs. As they reached the crest, Tamara realized her sandal's might cause her to slip descending the other side. She carefully placed each step, while Bijou ran, propelling her forward.

The next thing she knew, she was flat on her bottom, blood gushing from her forehead. She looked up into Hannah's face for an answer as to what had just happened, but Hannah simply stared at her, as the scene around Tamara started to come into focus.

The looming side of a semi-truck parked flush against the other side of the shrubs, now came into full view. Tamara saw Bijou under the semi, panting happily. The dog had pulled her headlong into the parked truck, which knocked her silly and split open her head.

Hannah took off her blue plaid flannel and wrapped it around Tamara's head. "Do you want me to take Bijou on ahead to the Groomers for his flea dip?"

"Uh, Hannah, I think that can wait. I believe I need to go to the hospital for stitches."

Her friend walked with her to the medical center on the other side of their complex, then took her dog home.

While she waited to be seen, Tamara had a rush of emotions. She was in physical pain but needed more than stitches. She ached for comfort. She was unable to reach Janet, so she called Grayson.

"Hi Grayson, I hate to bother you, but I was wondering if you would please go and wake up Janet for me? I need to talk to her, it's important."

"Sorry Tamara, I am in the middle of something. Just leave Janet a message, I'm sure she will get back to you when she can." he said.

As she hung up the phone, she felt the familiar sting of loneliness.

When she finally saw the Dr., she noticed how kind his eyes were. Before he started stitching, he paused and said in the most tender voice, "I am so sorry this happened to you."

Tears slipped down Tamara's face. It was like her Heavenly Father spoke those words to her through this kind man.

CHAPTER 45

May the Lord grant that each of you will find rest in the home of
another husband.
~ Ruth 1:9 NIV

AFTER SIX LONG YEARS OF NAVIGATING SINGLE MOTHERHOOD,
Tamara was immersed in a worship service at church when that
familiar still small voice arose. *"It's time to take your guard down, so I can
bring Boaz."*

As she made her way through the people, she saw a familiar face
headed towards her.

"Ron!" Tamara smiled. "What are you doing here? I have not
seen you in years! I didn't even know you went to church!"

"Hey Tamara, I got saved a year ago. I thought I would check
this church out, and can't believe that I am running into you. You
are beautiful as ever!" Ron exclaimed.

"That is so awesome that you know Jesus as Lord! Welcome to
the family! Wow, and to think, you were one of Brent's favorite
drinking buddies!" said Tamara.

"Goes to show you how powerful God is, huh Tamara? Let me take you to breakfast and we can catch up."

Tamara jotted down her phone number and gave it to Ron. In the foyer, she noticed Elaine and caught up to her.

"Elaine, you are not going to believe this. A man from my past was here this morning. He says he got saved, I hope it's true. He wants to take me out for breakfast, but I am scared!"

"What are you afraid of Tamara? Trust the work God has done in you. You won't be deceived again. Trust Him."

Elaine prayed with Tamara and sent her on her way. She shared the word the Lord had spoken during worship; how the timing was so strange for Ron to show up, right as God told her to drop her guard for Boaz to come.

∼

TAMARA HAD JUST CLIMBED INTO BED, WHEN THE PHONE RANG. IT was Ron. "You aren't going to bail on me for our breakfast date, are you?"

"Now why would I do that Ron?" she laughed.

"I guess I am just paranoid. I can see why you might be afraid of seeing me. I have always had a crush on you, Tamara. I actually asked Brent permission to date you if you two ever divorced."

"What? I did not know that. You dated most of my friends but never seemed to even notice me."

"Oh, I noticed you, but then Brent came into the picture and I knew he'd kill me if he knew. But one night when you guys were fighting, he told me he was done with you. That's when I asked him if I could pursue you if you guys divorced. He said he could care less. He was pretty drunk and high, and was checking out some girl." said Ron.

"I'm sure he was. I am so thankful to be free of him! I became too much of a Bible thumper for you anyway. I remember talking to you about Jesus and you always blew me off!"

"How could I forget? Some of it must have stuck, because here I am! Born again. Maybe God has brought us back together, for a reason." he said.

"Who knows? But I want you to know, I think it is amazing that you got saved, and I can't wait to hear all about it. But we need to finish this conversation in the morning, I am beat! Goodnight Ron."

"Goodnight Tamara, God Bless."

While she drifted off into sleep, she prayed, *God, did you bring this man to me?*

~

TAMARA ARRIVED ON TIME AT THE CUTE LITTLE BAVARIAN restaurant in town. She felt peaceful since Elaine had prayed and reassured her, and Ron was nice enough on the phone, yet an uneasiness started to rise.

Five, ten minutes passed as she continued to glance towards the doors. *God, why is he late? If he is a wolf in sheep's clothing, please show me!* she prayed silently.

She smiled at the Hostess behind the cash register. What she saw next left her completely undone. Next to the base of the cash register lay a porcelain figurine of a grey and white wolf.

"Tamara, so sorry I am late!" Ron's words startled her into the present. Shaken to the core, Tamara rose from the bench, accepting Ron's hand.

They made small talk and ordered breakfast. As she prayed in the spirit, the cool, confident and handsome man who had approached her at church all but disappeared. Ron seemed nervous as a cat, fidgeting with his silverware and napkin. It did not escape Tamara's notice that he dove right into his plate when it came without so much as a prayer.

Mustering up a boldness in her spirit, she looked him square in the face. "So, Ron, tell me about how you came to receive Jesus as Lord of your life."

Looking away, Ron grabbed the pepper shaker. "I, just you know, believe we all have a higher power. It's how I stopped drinking."

"Jesus is not just a higher power Ron; He is God Almighty." she said.

"Uh, yeah. I believe that too." said Ron.

The meal became unbearably awkward as Ron rambled on about Alcoholics Anonymous and the Twelve steps, never looking Tamara in the eye for more than a brief second.

"I wish you the best Ron, it was nice to see you again. You take care." Tamara said, heading for her car.

"Maybe I will see you around church, or we can go to a movie sometime?" Ron called after her.

"Yeah, I might see you at church, but I am not dating. See you later." Tamara waved goodbye and drove away.

She never saw or heard from him again.

⁓

A FEW WEEKS LATER TAMARA'S FRIEND ELAINE ASKED IF SHE'D LIKE to visit the church plant where she was leading worship. She wanted Tamara to meet the guitar player.

Sunday morning, Elaine pointed the guitar player out before the service started. He was setting up the stage. He was unlike any of the men Tamara had dated in the past. There was no arrogance about him. She had been prompted by the Holy Spirit to tear up her list of the *perfect guy*.

The guitarist was a handsome man, clean cut with dark hair and glasses; but a bit "churchier" than she was used to.

After the service Elaine introduced them.

"Hi, I'm Micah." He said with a grin that lit up his face.

She was impressed with his genuine smile. He looked into her eyes as if he saw her, not just physically, but into her soul.

"Did Micah ask for my phone number Elaine?" Tamara asked on their way home.

"Yes, I gave him your phone number. I figured it would be okay with you."

"Yes, that's fine, he seems to be very nice."

Two days went by and Tamara became upset. Why wasn't he calling?

Didn't he think she was pretty? Every insecurity she'd ever had, surfaced.

~

THE FOLLOWING WEDNESDAY, WHILE GETTING READY FOR BED, THE phone rang. "Hi Tamara, this is Micah. It was nice to meet you the other day. I was wondering if you'd like to meet somewhere for coffee or dinner?"

"Hi Micah, I would like that very much. I am open to going to dinner. Where did you have in mind?"

"How about that little place off Broadway, The Cottage, this Friday night?"

"Oh, I love that place! What time would you like to meet?"

"I get off work at five, so how about six?"

"Six on Friday night sounds perfect, I look forward to getting to know you."

"Me too, you have a nice evening Tamara."

"Thank you, Micah, see you Friday."

She really didn't want to get off the phone so quickly, she loved the sound of his voice.

~

THEY SAT AT A TINY TABLE WITH A CROCHETED TABLECLOTH IN THE cozy little restaurant, the atmosphere and aroma of homemade bread set the stage nicely for an intimate conversation. It was as if God blanketed the table with His favor. There were no awkward pauses or lack of things to say. They shared from their hearts and the evening was over before they knew it. Micah had to cut the night short, he had to get up early the next morning to leave for a retreat out of town. They said their goodbyes and Tamara wondered...*is it him*?

When Micah got back into town, he called Tamara and asked

her out on another date. She enjoyed their time together but was skittish, still a bit afraid of being duped again.

After each date, they prayed together and Micah spoke into her life in a way no man ever had. He'd answer the questions of her heart she'd never asked anyone but God. He did not pressure her physically, honoring her vow to never kiss another man until it was the one whom she would marry.

Micah called one sunny afternoon and asked her to go on a hike with the church singles group, then asked what she was doing that weekend, and the following one.

She panicked! "Micah, that is so nice of you to think of me, but I don't know what the boys and I are doing that far in advance. Maybe I will see you at the hike?"

"Oh, sure. I didn't mean to upset you."

"Oh, I am not upset. I have been a bit overwhelmed lately though, lots going on. Bye."

～

SHE CALLED HER FRIEND ELAINE, "HE'S COMING ON TOO STRONG!"

"I thought you wanted to get married." Elaine pointed out.

"I do but..."

"You don't know what you want, do you? Well, you'd better decide, because he's a good one." Said Elaine.

Tamara brushed it aside, and got ready to go on the church hike. During the hike Tamara missed Micah. She thought he'd show up, but when he didn't it upset her.

She realized she was really falling for this guy.

It was Tamara's turn to call Micah.

His stepping back was exactly what she needed to hear her own heart. When his voice came over the message machine, she sighed. She really liked his voice. "Hi Micah, it's Tamara. Missed you on the hike, I was wondering if you would like to come over tonight?"

He came over that evening.

"So, Micah, why didn't you show up for the hike on Saturday?"

"You know Tamara, I really wanted to go and see you but God

told me to honor your wishes and be patient with you. He reminded me that love does not seek its own way."

Tamara's heart melted, men had quoted the Bible to her before, but Micah's words rang true.

～

THE NEXT DAY SHE FELT THE LORD'S INVITATION TO GO SIT IN THE yard and read First Corinthians 13. She'd read from this chapter many years, and it had always devastated her. She had never, in her entire life, been loved like this chapter described.

She sat in the warmth of the sun, reading, when she heard God's voice in her spirit, *"As you read it this time, think of the way Micah has been towards you."*

"Love is patient, love is kind...." Warm tears trickled down her cheeks, "It does not envy, it does not boast, it is not proud, it is not rude, it is not self-seeking, it is not easily angered, it keeps no record of wrongs. Love does not delight in evil but rejoices in the truth. It always protects, always trusts, always hopes, and always perseveres."

Her Prince had come.

～

A MONTH LATER, MICAH TOOK TAMARA OUT FOR A ROMANTIC dinner, followed by a drive along the water. He parked the car, and the conversation flowed as easily as the river. They were about to end their evening together with prayer, when Micah got very quiet. After a few moments, he spoke softly,

"Tamara...I don't want to scare you but..."

Tamara felt a surge of love from his hand that swept over her entire being, she knew what his next words would be.

"I love you." He said.

Tamara paused, too overcome by emotion to speak, but eventually whispered, "I know...and I love you too."

A few nights later Micah came for dinner and after the dishes were done, they talked privately.

Tamara stumbled over her next words, "Today I had to fill out an emergency card for Joshua's daycare and I put you down as the contact person, I'm so embarrassed to say this but...."

"What?" Micah asked.

"The part of the card where it asked how you were related to me; I wrote down that you were my fiancée." Her cheeks flushed and she looked away.

Micah grabbed her chin and turned her face back to him, "Well, I was actually going to ask you to marry me tonight," He took her hands in his, "Tamara, will you do me the honor of becoming my wife?"

"Oh, yes!" Tamara threw her arms around him and kissed him for the very first time.

Tamara felt something physically lay down to rest in her soul, something she had never felt before. The prayer of Naomi for Ruth in the Bible was answered again, to find rest in a husband.

The final confirmation. Micah was her Boaz.

∾

FOUR MONTHS AFTER THEIR ENGAGEMENT, THEY WERE MARRIED AND God was in each and every detail.

"It's perfect Tamara. You look beautiful!" Janet exclaimed.

"Oh, but it is too expensive!" Tamara sighed.

She did feel like a Princess in the wedding dress. The top was intricately woven with lace and pearls. Long lacy sleeves came to a point on her hand. The empire waist complimented her figure, as cascades of champagne silk flowed to the floor.

"You can make payment's Tamara, you have to get it, it's the one!"

"You are right, it is the one!" Tamara squealed. "I will take it!" she said to the sales clerk.

∾

THE CRISP NOVEMBER DAY SEEMED CUSTOM ORDERED; THE RAINS

held back by a canopy of sunshine. Tamara knew God was smiling on their wedding day.

The finishing touches were coming together at the church, as Tamara got ready in a room upstairs.

"Can you believe it Janet? The day is finally here!"

"I know, I am so happy for you girlfriend! You are beautiful! You are positively glowing! Do you need anything else before I go down? I want to check in on the boys before I get seated."

"No, I am good, Thank you so much for everything. You taking the boys for our Honeymoon is above and beyond." Tamara said.

"Are you kidding me? I am their Auntie Janet, and I already bought lots of goodies and movies to keep them entertained. We will have a wonderful time together! I love you so much! This is your day! I will see you downstairs."

"I love you too!" Tamara said as she hugged her best friend.

Upon final inspection in the mirror, Tamara closed her eyes for a moment. *Thank you for this day, for Micah, for Your promises, for placing my son's and I in a family. Thank you, Abba.*

"People are starting to arrive Tamara." Elaine, her matron of honor entered, handing her a water bottle.

"How are the boys doing? Do you think the guys are helping them get into their tuxes okay?" Tamara asked.

"They are just fine Tamara, don't you worry about a thing, we have everything under control."

Music streamed through the door. "You ready Tamara?" asked Elaine.

"Yes, I am *so* ready."

Tamara tried not to smudge her make up already, but it was not going to be easy. The church was everything she had hoped, adorned with Burgundy and White flowers, and Hunter Green foliage.

Brandon walked up and took Tamara's arm. "Ready Mom?"

"Yes, my brown eyed handsome man. Thank you for walking me down the aisle. I love you so much!"

"I love you too Mom. You look beautiful."

Micah's nephew Brian sat at the Baby Grand, playing a jazzy

version of *Here Comes the Bride* as Brandon escorted her to the front of the church.

Tamara's eye swept over the guests faces as she walked. *You all look so beautiful,* she thought. *And, look at you my sweet Aaron!* Never one to sport more than an old T-shirt and shorts, he now stood proud in his Tux. Leaning out of the aisle, he whispered, "Hey mom! You look great."

Joshua stood next to Micah in matching tux. He greeted his Mom with dimpled smile, fists held tightly to the ring bearer pillow.

She locked eyes with her groom, and simultaneously broke out in tears. "You look so handsome!" she mouthed.

"You're beautiful!" he mouthed back.

"Who gives this woman to this man?" The Pastor began.

"We do, Tamara's sons." Said Brandon.

The Pastor welcomed everyone and thanked them for coming. He shared a few words on marriage, and a short testimony of how God had brought them together. Then he gave the guests an opportunity.

"Tamara and Micah would like their wedding to include an invitation to another wedding, The Wedding Supper of the Lamb. All you have to do is confess your need of Jesus Christ as Lord and Savior, to save you from your sin. Believe that He is God, who came to earth in the form of a man, lived a sinless life, died on a cross for your sins, and rose again. If you would like to do this, please bow your heads with me in prayer."

The Presence of God encompassed the room.

Micah quietly walked to the side of the stage and picked up his guitar. He turned to Tamara and began serenading her with the most beautiful love song she had ever heard.

Tamara and Micah exchanged their personally written vows and were pronounced man and wife.

Tamara's matron of honor prayed prophetically over their union.

"God's blessings are not only going to chase you down; they will overtake you."

CHAPTER 46

MAKE US GLAD FOR AS MANY DAYS AS YOU HAVE AFFLICTED US, FOR as many years as we have seen trouble. May your deeds be shown to your servants, your splendor to their children. May the favor of the Lord our God rest on us; establish the work of our hands for us— yes, establish the work of our hands. ~Psalm 90:15-27 NIV

TAMARA AND MICAH'S HONEYMOON WAS INCREDIBLE IN EVERY WAY. Making love, not just another lust filled encounter, was an experience beyond anything she could have imagined. Tamara truly felt like a blushing virginal bride, and although her body bore the marks of three children, when Micah looked upon her, she became undone, as he told her how beautiful she was. She saw the truth of it in his eyes. She had a revelation through a man's eyes for the very first time, how God must see her through the blood of Christ, without spot or blemish.

Sunday morning, they sought out a church in the town where they were staying. At the end of the service, the Pastor and his wife prophesied promises and spoke a blessing over them. Incredibly, after all of the spiritual abuse Tamara had endured through false prophesies, she was still open to receive the ministry of the gifts of the Spirit.

As they worshipped, God's Presence overtook them and Tamara had a vision of a female twirling and dancing with a little baby girl uplifted in her arms.

"Is that me as a baby Lord? Are you healing me from birth?" she asked.

The vision panned around like a camera, revealing her own face as the woman holding the child.

You will have a daughter and she will bring healing to your life and to many others.

≈

A YEAR AND A HALF LATER, SHE WAS PREGNANT. AN ULTRASOUND confirmed that they were indeed having a girl! Micah and Tamara could not decide on a name. One afternoon while paying a bill over the phone, she was put on hold. Filling the empty time, Tamara asked God, *what do you want to name our daughter?*

"I want to name her Charity Lynn." Tamara announced over dinner.

"Charity Lynn, okay. Yeah, I like it." said Micah.

"You better, since God gave me the name!" she laughed.

The day of Tamara's birthday, she had an appointment for a stress test for baby, who was due that very week. She called her best friend, who had moved away.

"Hi, Janet...is there any way that you can come to town early? Micah is working and I don't want to go to my appointment alone..." she dissolved into tears.

"Hold on, I'm coming, my bags are already packed!" came Janet's voice over the phone.

≈

"THANK YOU FOR COMING JANET. I DON'T MEAN TO BE SUCH A MESS;

it is just so hard for me not to be able to have my parents come and meet the baby. It's my birthday and I just felt so alone!"

"But Tamara, you know they are not safe. Remember, your Pastor had that vision of your mom holding out her hands, like she couldn't wait to get her hands on that baby!" Janet said.

"Yeah, I know, but still, it's *so* hard!" said Tamara.

"And don't forget, if you had not left her web of deceit, you would not even have Charity!"

"Truer words have never been spoken Janet. I am even having mixed feelings about Terri coming. I know she said she came back to the Lord, but I can't shake an uneasy feeling!"

"I do not trust her for a minute Tamara. I know you want to believe people when they say they are looking for God, but your family has always been so deceptive!"

"Well, I promised her that we would let her know when the baby is here, so I have to at *least* call her."

During the stress test monitoring of baby's heart rate, the attending nurse dropped the paper feed coming out of the machine and ran from the room. Startled, Tamara looked frantically at Janet, who immediately spoke truth into her. "Tamara, you know God's promises for this child. You know everything will be just fine. Now let's pray!"

Prayer calmed Tamara and changed the atmosphere of the room. When the nurse returned, she reassured them that everything would be okay, but they needed Tamara to check into a room, as the baby was pressing on the umbilical cord.

"Hi Micah,"

"You still at the appointment? How did it go?" he asked.

"Yeah, I am still at the hospital, they checked me in. The baby is showing some signs of stress…" she cried.

"Don't worry honey, I'm leaving work. I will be right there!"

MICAH RUSHED TO HIS WIFE'S SIDE, "I'M HERE BABE, YOU KNOW GOD is taking care of our baby, do you need anything?"

"No. Now that you are here, I don't need another thing."

After a full day of labor, the baby was close to making her appearance. Janet had taken Tamara's boys home to feed them and get some rest, while Micah settled in for a nap on a small couch in the labor room.

The nurse checked Tamara and let her know she may be giving birth within the next hour or two. Tamara woke up her husband. She pleaded with him to ask the Dr. for an epidural. She had always opted for natural birth, but not this time.

Micah left the room to get a nurse and call Janet to get to the hospital with the boys.

The nurse came and checked Tamara's progress. She agreed that it was time to order the epidural.

It seemed an eternity before Micah rejoined his wife and whispered into her ear,

"You are not going to be able to have the epidural, there is an emergency and the lady in the next room needs the anesthesiologist."

Tamara was quite upset; she was so tired of fighting through pain.

Micah pulled Tamara from her selfish thoughts. "Honey, we need to pray, It's serious. Both their lives are in danger!"

They prayed together for the unknown woman and her child.

"How are you doing Tamara? Do you need anything? I'm here now, the boys are in the waiting room." said Janet.

"I'm good, but can you do me a favor and call my sister? She wanted to be here once the baby was close to being delivered."

"If you are sure, I will call her."

Tamara nodded. Janet walked over to the phone beside the hospital bed. The Dr. rushed into the room and checked Tamara. "Hang that phone up. Now!" barked the Dr. at Janet.

"Okay Tamara, now push!" said the Dr.

Two pushes later, the baby shot out like a cannon. Her daughter's cry brought tears of joy. The love for her child was overwhelming. She looked into her husband's eyes, "Isn't she perfect honey?" he smiled in agreement.

"How are the lady and her baby doing in the next room?" she asked.

Micah shook his head, "It's not good. The baby didn't make it."

Her Dr. had come from delivering a stillborn, to delivering her precious baby.

Exhausted from labor, it was so hard to process, but her boys storming into the room to meet their sister pulled joy back to the forefront.

"She's cool lookin Mom." said Aaron.

"Can I hold her?" asked Joshua.

Brandon had already swept his sister up and was rocking her in the chair next to the bed. Tamara laid her head back on her pillow, an uneasiness suddenly coming upon her. She noticed a dark billowy cloud creeping into the room at the ceiling level. She didn't have her contacts in, so she squinted to see who had come into the room.

She heard her sister's constricted voice, "So, why didn't anybody call me to be here for the birth?"

The anger shifted the peaceful atmosphere and Tamara kicked into her old role as peacemaker.

"Oh Terri, I am so sorry, Janet picked the phone up to call you right before Charity was born but the Doctor told her to put the phone down."

A divine intervention.

Terri made a few comments about how beautiful the baby was and tersely made a quick exit. Tamara prayed protection under her breath the entire time her sister was there. She could not let her guard down in her family's presence.

Tamara dressed Charity for the first time, pulling silky arms through tiny dress sleeves. She wept with joy, believing that Charity would never go through the suffering she had known. She caressed her baby soft cheek; this face would never know the harsh slap of a hand. She ran her fingers through sweet little curls, never to be pulled in anger from her head.

Charity would be raised in a world that Tamara had only dreamed of.

~

WHEN CHARITY WAS ABOUT 6 MONTHS OLD, TAMARA BUNDLED HER up and went with Janet to a neighborhood Frozen Yogurt Shop. As they stood in line, Tamara adjusted the white, lacy bonnet on her daughter and turned to Janet, "It's so hard to not let my parents meet Charity. I pray and talk with Micah, to see what he thinks about it, but he never has a peace about opening that door. But I know that God can change the hardest heart. He changed us!"

"Yes, he did Tamara, but your family never repents. They talk heaven and live like hell!"

A strong putrid smell suddenly filled the establishment.

"Do you smell that?" Tamara covered her nose.

"Yes, *gross*!!"

They both scanned the floor to see if a patron had gotten sick.

That was when they saw her.

Terri had just walked in. She met their gaze and strode boldly up to her sister. They had not talked since that day in the hospital. Janet scooped up the car seat holding baby Charity.

Terri and Tamara made awkward small talk while Janet took the baby with her to find a table. Terri left within a few minutes, the smell of vomit going with her.

A Proverb sprang forth in Tamara's spirit.

"As a dog returns to his vomit, so a fool repeats his folly." Proverbs 26:11

~

TAMARA WATCHED HER HUSBAND PICK THEIR DAUGHTER UP AS IF SHE was the most valuable china, and it never failed to move her. Charity grew and Tamara was shocked at herself for being jealous. She had become quite upset at her sister-in-law Jean when she'd shared how having a daughter would be bittersweet due to Tamara's abusive background. At the time she could not even fathom what Jean was talking about, but now she was starting to understand. She had to reconcile the fact that she never knew that kind of Daddy, and it still hurt.

Tamara opened a daycare in her home to supplement their income. The thought of leaving the daughter she had longed for and work outside her home, was incomprehensible to her. She reached out to the single mom's in her church, empathizing with their struggle to provide. She offered them a safe and loving environment for their children, at minimal cost. Long days with five children under five years old, left her exhausted, but she was happy.

One day when Micah came home, he hung up his coat as she flew by with a raspy, "How was your day?"

He caught her hand and sat her down, with a concerned look on his face. "Honey, are you okay? Is it your throat again?"

"Yeah, I think I am coming down with a cold." she said.

"You say that every time, but then after a day or two, you are fine. It happens a lot!" he said.

"I guess I have a really good immune system that fights off the colds!" she smiled wearily and gathered the belongings of the youngest child she watched.

"Melanie late again tonight?" he asked.

"Yes, she can't help it, her boss makes her stay over."

"Tamara, you have got to be stricter with these mother's they are taking advantage of you!" Micah admonished.

"This is a ministry Micah, where is your compassion?"

"I know Tamara, but you need to take care of yourself and Charity, you have limits!"

Tamara crawled into bed past midnight, and prayed for her throat to be healed and strength to get up the next day and do it all again.

A week later, in the midst of the hustle and bustle of the children, Tamara clutched her constricted throat, "*God, what is this? Why does my throat hurt like this so often?*"

The answer was immediate, "*it is suppressed pain from your past.*"

The room started to swirl; her soul felt as if she were shrinking into darkness. Even the smallest request of a child overwhelmed her.

She started to panic.

She grabbed the phone and dialed an elderly woman she had met in a Bible study, who had taken her under her wing in the past few months.

"Deana, can you please come over and sit with the children for a bit? I don't feel well, something is terribly wrong."

"Now Tamara," Deana responded calmly. "I will pray and see what God says and call you back."

Tamara hung up the phone in shock, did the woman not hear her plea? *God help me!*

The phone came off the hook into Tamara's hands before the first ring finished sounding. "Are you coming?" asked Tamara.

"No, God told me that you will be okay, I am not to come." Deana's monotone voice trailed off.

Unbelievable!

Tamara grabbed some snacks for the kids and turned on a Toddler show. She took a deep breath and dialed another friends number.

"Christine, can you please come for about an hour, I am sick and need to lay down but I have all of my daycare kids."

"Sure Tamara, I will be right over."

Tamara paced as she waited for her friend to get there, her angry thoughts consumed her. *Deana told me that she was my spiritual mother! Yet she won't come when I so desperately need her? What kind of mother doesn't come to her child?*

When Christine arrived, Tamara could barely speak, her throat was so bad. The tears running down her face said it all.

"You just go and rest Tamara, I have got everything under control!"

Tamara lay down on her bed, and drew her body into a fetal position. She sobbed into a pillow, muffling the sounds to not frighten the children. After crying for a long time, she lay exhausted and slipped into a dark place. Her legs started to push her body backwards. Suddenly, she was in a closet, hiding as far into the back of it as she could, she willed to disappear, pressing into the wall. Her father's hands were reaching for her, pulling on her dress, trying to drag her out.

"No! No! No!" Tamara cried out, catapulting herself into the present.

She *knew* it was true, and she was just three years old.

The next hour, God ministered to Tamara. The horrid memories that she had long suppressed of her own sexual abuse were now in the light. What had been done in the darkness would no longer hold her captive. Yet she still had so many questions. *"But God, why did my mother tell me that I was passed up, that I couldn't have handled such abuse? Why did she not allow me to heal along with my sister's and brother's? What kind of mom doesn't come to her child?"*

"Your mother's own pain and guilt were too much to bear, she couldn't face one more child's abuse." He whispered.

Victoria was the one who couldn't handle it.

Tamara's throat never constricted in pain again. In Christ, she could not only *handle it*, but overcome it!

～

CHARITY LYNN BECAME THE GLUE THAT BROUGHT TAMARA'S SONS and her new husband together as a family unit. The boys initially resisted Micah as their step-father.

One afternoon Joshua was being admonished by Micah and yelled, "You're not my father!"

"You're right Joshua, I'm not your father. But there are some things I can give you that your father cannot."

"Like what?!" Josh asked defiantly.

"I can teach you about the things of God, music and computers."

Joshua seemed satisfied with the answer and never challenged his stepfather's position in his life again.

～

EVEN AFTER YEARS OF RESTORATION, TAMARA STILL HAD TO CHOOSE to trust again, to hope in the body of Christ.

Lord Jesus, you have to guard my heart, you know that when I do church on my own, I build walls or let harmful things in. You are the gatekeeper of my heart and I trust you alone with it.

TAMARA AND HER FAMILY FOUND A HEALTHY CHURCH AND THRIVED, yet the church was filled with imperfect people. There were still liars in the church and pockets of deception. However, sitting right next to Tamara and her family were the real thing; beautiful but flawed children of God, she being one of them. There was even still betrayal and rejection to deal with, not at all what she expected.

The Bible told her plainly that there would be wheat and tares in the church until the Lord's Angels separated them in the end. So why was it that she was continually shocked when she discerned it?

And, was her discernment correct?

She realized that God left the separating to the Angels for that very reason; so much damage would happen if everyone shouted *Tare* once they saw a bad day or even season in anyone's life.

God had taught her that only eyes filled with love can truly discern. When she saw that some people were toxic, although she may not be able to be in close relationship, she still must contend and pray with hope for change. Loving her enemies, blessing those who cursed her, and praying for those who mistreated her, as Jesus commanded, did not mean she was to stay in abusive relationships or cultivate them.

When she felt she did not have the strength to cross the threshold of a church, the Lord sweetly wooed her, *Will you go for me?*

Tamara could never resist Him. She rose from her slump, and headed for the Church doors. With each obedient step, she experienced more freedom and joy, that overshadowed any hesitation.

She realized, until Christ's return, she would not have the Family of perfection that she longed for. She ached for the Kingdom of God in its wholeness, and Holiness. Perhaps she was sensing yet another inkling of fellowshipping in Christ's suffering.

CHAPTER 47

DO NOT THINK THAT I HAVE COME TO BRING PEACE TO THE EARTH. I have not come to bring peace, but a sword. For I have come to set a man against his father, and a daughter against her mother, and a daughter-in-law against her mother-in-law. And a person's enemies will be those of his own household. Whoever loves father or mother more than me is not worthy of me, and whoever loves son or daughter more than me is not worthy of me. And whoever does not take his cross and follow me is not worthy of me. Whoever finds his life will lose it, and whoever loses his life for my sake will find it. ~Matthew 10:34-39 ESV

DRIVING BACK TO HER HOMETOWN WAS SURREAL. AARON MOVED back in with his Dad to be with the friends he had grown up with. He wanted to graduate with his class. Watching Aaron play football used to be such a fun time for Tamara, but tonight she would have to stand before the townspeople on the field to receive a rose from Aaron, a Senior on the Football team.

"I feel faint Micah! I don't know if I can go in front of all those people. They judged me so long ago, they have no idea who I really am!"

"Honey, it's been nine years. Do you really think anybody is going to even remember?"

"They will too remember Micah! We were in the Newspaper! Small towns don't forget their gossip!"

"Relax Tamara, they can't do anything to you."

"I know, you are right. I am only here for Aaron anyway. I need to concentrate on that."

They approached the overcrowded stadium, scanning the bleachers for a seat. Suddenly, Brent and his father approached them.

"We've saved a spot for you." Brent grinned.

Stunned, Tamara and Micah walked the length of the stadium, paraded before those who had judged her guilty of being an unfit mother all those years before.

She glanced at her former captor Brent before she sat down. She saw the smug look on his face, as if he were showing everyone it had all been a lie, and Tamara had finally come around.

At Aaron's graduation ceremony a few months later, Tamara felt queasy while walking into that same stadium. She felt prepared through much prayer for what she might face, but still something was unsettling. She hugged her son and congratulated him after the ceremony. Brent and his girlfriend pushed their way into the circle, and as if things weren't awkward enough, she saw Victoria approaching. It had been over 6 years since she had seen her mother.

Panic gripped Tamara. She leaned into her husband and Janet, desperately whispering, "Are you praying?"

"Of course we are!" Janet assured her.

Micah turned to greet his estranged mother-in-law.

"So, you're Tamara's husband," Victoria sized him up, but her attention soon diverted to Charity in Tamara's arms.

"Oh, can I hold her?" she asked. Before Tamara could respond, her mother was stroking her daughter's face, cooing softly, "I'm your Grandma sweetie."

Charity burrowed into her mother's arms, shunning the embrace of her Grandmother.

"Mom, she's tired." Tamara said inching away.

"Oh, I understand, she doesn't know me yet, but she will!" Victoria declared confidently.

"Well Mom, we need to get on the road, Micah has to get up early for work."

"But you will call me so we can get together for lunch, right? We can't be apart forever. The Devil can't win." Victoria pleaded.

"Yeah Mom, I will call you sometime."

Tamara noticed how quiet her usually chatty daughter was since they left the event. She turned and looked at Charity, she looked ashen.

"Mommy, I'm sick." Charity spoke weakly.

How could I let this happen?

Tamara repented for letting her mom come near her child. "We have to pray!" Tamara shouted. "I rebuke the spirit of death, you cannot touch my child, in Jesus name!"

Micah joined in the prayers as Janet laid hands on Charity for healing. Immediately her daughter's color returned and she was absolutely fine.

"It was Victoria's touch! I let her touch Charity! I let my guard down in that moment because I felt sorry for her." Tamara sobbed.

"Don't be so hard on yourself Tamara, I felt compassion for her too." Micah said, trying to comfort his wife.

"The strong boundaries that you set in place are not too harsh Tamara. I know how much you have struggled with them. They are God's protection for your whole family. You cannot let your mother near here." Janet counseled.

"You are so right! Forgiveness of my birth family is essential, but reconciliation is not possible!" Tamara agreed.

Tamara rocked her daughter to sleep, praying and singing over her until late that evening. She tiptoed out of her bedroom, and went into the living room and pulled out an old family album. Scanning the pictures, she came across one from a Thanksgiving dinner years before; A large table laden with decadent food, surrounded by people. Tamara felt as if she had come upon a stranger's photo album. Her eyes rested on each face of her relatives. They were all familiar but somehow removed from her.

"*You have lost your life Tamara.*" she heard the Lord whisper.

In following Jesus, she had truly lost the life she had grown up in.

Every single excruciating step was worth it to find her life in Christ Jesus. The Lord before her, the world behind her, no turning back.

EPILOGUE

They built the high places of Baal in the Valley of the Son of Hinnom, to offer up their sons and daughters to Molech, though I did not command them, nor did it enter into My mind, that they should do this abomination to cause Judah to sin.
~Jeremiah 32:35 ESV

Tamara and her family prayed for idolatry to be brought down in their lives. They studied the Old Testament and saw how the kings time and again refused to take down high places. The places where the people's idols were exalted above the one true God. Therefore, the idolatry of the Israelites continued.

Victoria taught her children these truths, but when it came to bringing down her own idol, Sam, she would not. Even if it cost the very lives of her children.

In the book of Jeremiah, the Israelites were forbidden to practice the heathen customs such as, offering their children as burnt offerings to the false god Molech.

Tamara knew she and her siblings were laid at the feet of their mother's idol. And she had unwittingly followed in her footsteps, until God's divine intervention.

Tamara and her children had been passed through fire; the burning hot fires of incest, alcoholism, drug addiction, beatings, spiritual and emotional torment. By God's grace, they would not smell of smoke. Having been washed by the water of the Word, the fragrance of Christ would be released, to permeate future generations.

~

They triumphed over him by the blood of the Lamb and by the word of their testimony; they did not love their lives so much as to shrink from death. Rev 12:11

ABOUT THE AUTHOR

Jamie Sagerser has taught and facilitated Bible studies for over 30 years. She has served on women's ministry boards, done public speaking, and was on staff at a local church as the Pastoral Care Director. Since re-dedicating her life to Jesus Christ 33 years ago, it has been her passion, in an age of unprecedented deception, to reconcile people to the one true God.

Jamie and her husband Bob enjoy living in the beautiful Pacific Northwest, and have four children and 10 grandchildren.

Made in the USA
Coppell, TX
26 November 2019